HAMMER DOWN

HAMMER DOWN

DISCOVERING YOUR BEST

KP HALEY

Par 3, Inc.
Oklahoma City, OK

Published by Par 3, Inc., Oklahoma City, Oklahoma
First edition: December 2019

ISBN: 978-1-7340519-0-2 (hardback)
ISBN: 978-1-7340519-1-9 (paperback)
ISBN: 978-1-7340519-2-6 (ebook)

Library of Congress Control Number: 2019914207

Visit the author's website at kphaleyauthor.com.

To all first responders and defenders of our freedom ~
Thank you.

For my son, Dalton ~
Follow your dreams and live Hammer Down!

Table of Contents

The trouble is, we think we have time.

—Jack Kornfield

Introduction

My earliest memory is of my Grandpa Haley carrying me home from church, which was located right next door to our home. We left before the service began, because at three years old, I was fussy and misbehaving. Grandma stayed behind to attend the service, as she did every Sunday. When we entered the house, Grandpa gently set me down. Then, without a sound, he knelt down beside the couch, laid his head on his folded arms, and quietly and peacefully passed away. I spent about an hour with my grandpa, toddler-talking and surrounding him with pillows, which I transported from the next room using my little red tricycle. The moment my grandmother arrived is where my memory ceases. However, those final few precious minutes with my grandpa are remarkably vivid. Over a half century later, when I stop to think back on this person who was such a big part of my early days and then suddenly gone forever, I now realize this experience played a major role in shaping my life.

Even as a little kid, I recall having a tendency to approach things from a somewhat diplomatic and philosophical point of view. As the youngest of four boys, it may have been my way of trying to defuse my older brothers' attempts to entertain themselves at my expense, or perhaps it was our father's optimism and "roll with it" attitude that was passed along in my DNA.

Regardless, at the ripe old age of ten, I began the sport of wrestling, hoping that I might learn how to defend myself from my mob of older brothers. Admittedly, at first, I did not love wrestling. I'm not sure if it was because the coach had the attitude of a pissed off Marine drill sergeant just rejected from Parris Island, or because I sucked and was getting rolled up every day. That first year was misery. I won only one match and going to practice with that coach was a hell of a lot worse than my siblings' horseplay.

Once my brothers and I had started a sport season we were never allowed to quit, so I was going to finish my first year but did not plan to wrestle the following year. However, as we entered fifth grade, my buddy Troy decided he was going to wrestle. The only other sport available was basketball, which was not my forte or his. If my friend was willing to go through all the abuse and torture of wrestling again, I made the hard choice that I could, too. So, there we went, back to the crazy coach and back to getting choked out every day. Honestly, that second year wasn't much better. Amazingly, by the third year, with an awesome new coach, I began to win a few matches. I eventually became a proficient wrestler and even won a few tournaments along the way, although, like a lot of other good high school wrestlers, I was never able to win that coveted state champion title I wanted so badly.

I learned many things from enduring those early years and staying with that tough sport, mostly about myself. First, I learned that I was capable of taking and dishing out much more than I ever thought possible. I also discovered that I had a knack for coaching and motivating people. When I would attend wrestling camps, I'd come back and show the team the moves and techniques I'd learned. It was a good feeling knowing that I could help teach and inspire my teammates and maybe even help them improve and win. I decided I wanted to become a wrestling coach and earned a degree to do just that.

Ultimately however, I pursued and enjoyed a thirty-year career in the corporate world, first with Kraft Foods in retail sales and then as an agent with Oklahoma Farm Bureau Insurance. I eventually started my own insurance agency, which I later sold so I could explore other interests.

This book began as a few simple remarks written in my notebook on thoughts and suggestions I wish to highlight and pass along to my son, Dalton, who is now in his early twenties—tips for living life to the fullest, for being happier and healthier, and for finding peace. These are the things I would have liked someone to direct my attention toward when I was just starting out. In fact, these are the things I continue to reinforce within myself.

These tips and suggestions presented two very important opportunities for me. First, to encourage my son, and hopefully others, to not just dream, but to go after and *do* big, bold things in life. And second, it was simply the perfect goal to keep practicing that advice. The seed was planted, and it grew quickly.

The final decision to develop this work into the book you are now reading was made after noticing that many people—even the highly accomplished—seem to be living in a general state of boredom and unfulfillment. One would think with all the amazing and interesting places, people and topics to discover, and the ease with which we can now embark on such adventures of discovery, it would be just the opposite. I became very curious, okay maybe even obsessed, with learning more about this state of discontent. I began by contemplating some of the causes of unfulfillment and boredom: a sense of entitlement, unhappiness at work, lack of imagination, lack of appreciation for what one already has, lack of activity, the wrong activity, lack of goals, lack of self-esteem, too much free time, lack of hobbies and interests, lack of inspiration, lack of faith . . . The list could go on.

Now, I don't pretend to have all the answers or feel that I live above the fray, and in no way do I feel superior to anyone else. I only realize that, as with the wrestling camps I attended, I have learned some moves and acquired a bit of knowledge along the way that will prove useful to those interested in living a life filled with purpose and excitement.

This book is my humble attempt to share the things I have discovered to be effective and valuable in my own journey. I've tried to include some of the little things that I've found make a big difference, from small observations and practical techniques to timeless wisdom and truths. My hope is that you find the information within entertaining, useful and motivating in your quest to have purpose and inspiration in your daily life.

When you embrace and apply the principles laid out in these pages, you will begin to understand what the phrase "hammer down" really means. Implementing these powerful, time-proven methods is guaranteed to make positive changes that will propel you toward whatever target you choose. Do not underestimate the power of this approach—the results can and will be amazing! Stop settling for mediocrity, or worse. Apply these suggestions immediately and watch the positive forces go to work in your life.

This book is a call to action to participate, to expect success and to thrive in your daily life. Just like a bicycle, we are not much use until we get moving. Then we start to find our balance and begin to gain momentum. This is when great and amazing experiences can emerge. Nothing happens until you start pedaling, so get started now.

This book will show you how to get and keep the momentum working in your favor—so enjoy your journey; it's never too late and never too soon to begin.

ɧ

Chapter 1

Don't Skip the Hard Stuff

God pulled us out of the mud and set us on a dry hill.

—Rick Haley

Growing up, my three older brothers and I would see the occasional jet fly high overhead and every time imagine the passengers were escaping to some far-off tropical destination. Our particular environment required us to learn early on what responsibility and hard work were. Dad was a farmer and rancher as well as the local Farm Bureau insurance agent in our quiet little town of three hundred. While there are a few more folks now, Calumet was and still is a farming community, located between old Highway 66 and the south bank of the North Canadian River, fifty miles west of Oklahoma City. Our farm and ranch operation, Moonshine Bend, was two miles west of town and consisted of many acres of wheat, hay and river-bottom grassland. At the ranch headquarters we always had four or five horses in the pen, which we used to check and gather the three thousand head of cattle that were in the family feedlot.

My brother Tim used to say we lived on a work camp. The days were filled with loading and unloading semi-trucks of cows, corn and hay, working and branding the new cattle coming in, shipping the fat ones out, baling and hauling hay at all hours of the day and night, then doctoring all the sick animals, fixing fences, keeping all the equipment in working order, plowing the fields to prepare for planting, and grinding feed for all the livestock every day, rain or shine, holidays and Sundays. It was a lot of big work no matter how you sliced it up.

One cold and blustery winter day when I was twelve years old, my brother Rick and I were tasked with the wonderful job of grinding the hay and corn together and feeding each pen of cattle. With three thousand head of livestock this job had to be done daily, regardless of the weather conditions. On this particular morning the snow was coming down hard and everything was frozen solid with a quarter-inch-thick layer of ice from the night before. In these extreme conditions, it is vitally important for cattle to have good, high-protein feed and fresh water.

After a full day of working in miserably cold conditions, Rick and I were happily done grinding the last load of feed. As soon as we dumped it to the last bunch of heifers, we could finally get by the fire and warm up. As I stepped off the tractor to open the gate to the last pen, I noticed the cattle were all standing around the frost-free water tank using their tongues and the steam from their nostrils to try to melt the frozen-solid tank for a little drink. When I turned back, I saw Rick shaking his tightly bundled head back and forth in total disgust. He knew this meant no warmth for us until all the animals had fresh water.

It was after dark that evening before we had water running to that pen of cattle. This was after hours of digging in the frozen ground by hand to fix the busted water line, then thawing out the water tank with a propane burner. My brother later told me that we saved the lives of all those heifers.

I didn't realize it until later in life, but that day, and many more like it, had a big impact on my approach when dealing with difficult situations. You may have heard this saying before, but the philosophy is simple: "If you can't get out of it, then get into it with everything you got." In other words, "hammer down." I'm not saying you have to go out and save a cow's life, but you just might save your own.

Some things need to be done *now* and need to be done *right*. Had we not toughed it out that day, many animals would have gotten sick and died as a result. With farming and ranching comes much work and many risks—it is not for the faint of heart. However, it was the perfect environment to raise four sons and a prime training ground to develop and sharpen the "hammer down" attitude and techniques.

Many of our friends from town seemed to think we were rich, having all those cattle. I remember thinking, *Have you experienced the work it takes just to care for the family pet? Multiply that by three thousand and then square that number because of the size difference.* The ranching life may sound adventurous and even glamorous, and it was at times, but it was certainly not easy work.

In the summer of 1975, our dad bequeathed to my brother Tim and me matching International 856 tractors. No cab or air-conditioning of course, but we were happy to have canvas umbrellas attached to the fenders. They shook like hell but provided a spot of much needed and greatly appreciated shade. We would spend ten to twelve hours a day driving around and around in giant circles in those big fields, each time covering an eight-foot swath in a loud roar and a cloud of dust. Day after day of breathing and spitting up dirt. Then we'd move our tractors and implements to the next field and do it all over again.

At the end of each day, my brother and I, scrawny little shirtless kids that we were, looked like we had crawled straight out of the Dust Bowl. Our eyes, ears, and everything else were covered in a thick layer of grime. We would look at each other with little grins that quickly turned into full blown laughter because our teeth and the whites of our eyes were the only things that still shone clean.

The highlight of the day was stopping every couple of hours to wash the dust down with a drink from the water jug. I had a special trick of putting four juicy plums in my water jug and having one as a snack every couple of hours. I suppose even way back then I was using those plums to help break up and compartmentalize the day, which ended up making those dusty hours a little more bearable.

There are many amazing memories from my youth as well—like the countless times riding horseback with my dad, brothers, and our Grandpa Andy, who we called Gramp, looking out across the river that ran through our ranch. Or those mornings watching the dew lift and evaporate above the Bermuda grass as we rode to gather the cows and calves from the bottom pasture. And of course, there were the many, many times when things got real western—every day on the ranch seemed peppered with near misses, close calls, and, at times, direct hits.

Just thinking about one incident that my brother Rick survived makes my skin crawl. On this particular day, Rick was on his horse riding through a bunch of cattle that had been turned out in a little pasture below the hill from our ranch headquarters. As he was easing his horse through the small herd, he noticed a blind steer with a runny nose that needed attention. So, like he'd done a thousand times before, Rick roped the ill bovine and tended to it with the medical supplies he carried in his saddle bags.

As my brother finished doctoring the steer, he removed the rope and tossed it behind him, and he began to gather up the medicine. It was at this point that the not so sick animal got up and charged at my brother, knocking him backwards and forcing his right boot directly into the center of the rope loop lying on the ground. At that exact moment, the horse spooked from all the commotion and took off at full speed for the barn, dragging Rick by his right leg at the end of the rope. It is still terrifying to think about, even these many years later. My brother claims the only thing that saved his life that day was a mud hole he was drug through that made him all slippery and allowed a little less friction over the rough and rocky terrain. You should also know that Rick is tougher than the back wall at the gun range, which I am certain helped as well. He was dragged about a quarter mile, around farm implements and fence posts. Had one gate been turned the wrong way, he would have been pulled under it and ripped apart. Miraculously, though he lost a lot of the skin on his back and legs and spent a night in the hospital, within a few days he was back on his horse again, roping and doctoring cattle. And that's how we learned to roll—if you're not dead or busted up bad, you need to get up and push onward with whatever you got left.

Between managing his insurance agency, trading commodities, running the farm and ranch operation, and raising four wild boys, you might say our dad was the epitome of "hammer down." He always looked forward to Saturdays because, with no school, he had a full crew of us and plenty that needed to be done on the farm. This day was reserved for a full day's work around our operation. My brothers and I will never forget the highlight of those Saturdays: lunch. Our mom would always cook something amazing, and piles of it. After we finished eating, we were granted twenty minutes of shut-eye before it was back to work. We looked like a bunch of beached sea lions scattered around that living room floor. It takes a lot of food to feed three meals a day to five hungry guys, and this went on for years. Our mom cooked and cleaned and hauled us all over hell and back, to doctors, sports, and school, or any activity we could come up with that might get us off that damn work camp. In its own way, our mom's selflessness taught my brothers and me things about the "hammer down" principles that could not be learned by working in the fields.

Looking back at those days on the ranch, I believe one of the most important lessons we learned is that life is just a good daily dose of unexpected shit. Sometimes it's good shit and sometimes it's not so good. We learned to expect things to not work as planned, because they rarely ever did on the farm. Everywhere you turned was a flat tire, a burned-out bearing, or a new surprise to deal with. We learned to expect it, roll with it, and minimize what we could. We learned how to fix things and we learned how to pay attention so things didn't get torn up in the first place.

We were focused and driven. Mistakes cost work, money and—more important to us—time. Being efficient meant we could find time for other things; we only hoped it would not include rolling up barbed wire. As my oldest brother, Randy, likes to say, "Just handle it." And that's what we learned to do. We became efficient at handling the speed bumps of daily life on the farm.

As the youngest, if I wanted to tag along, I had to keep up and catch on quick. I saw and learned fast what the difficult stuff was. It took me a bit longer, however, to learn how to identify and appreciate what the good stuff was. Ironically, many times, the hard stuff *is* the good stuff. If the unexpected doesn't happen, you really don't have much to talk about. That's when life gets interesting. You see, the cattle's water freezing that evening was a shitstorm at the time; I would have chosen to be about anywhere else rather than lying in a cold and sloppy ditch, working on a busted water line in the spitting sleet and snow. Now, however, I appreciate and cherish more than gold that vivid memory of working alongside my brother in those extreme conditions.

The point is: don't skip over the hard stuff. Do what you have to do from the position you are in right now. Start and improve from there, even if that means getting in a muddy ditch in subfreezing weather. Be willing to do what you have to do when the time comes. Be deliberate and focused, whether it's going after your goals or dealing with the daily problems that continue to pop up. After thoughtful and careful consideration of the situation, be determined, take small steps forward, dig in and do what needs to be done.

Surviving, and thriving, in the face of extreme difficulty and overwhelming odds is where great stories, even legends and heroes, are born. When you approach a difficult situation with this in mind, you may even learn to welcome the unexpected hurdles. This shift in perspective allows you to meet challenges and obstacles with a clear head and few adverse reactive emotions. Not to mention, it helps make life a hell of a lot more fun.

ћ

Chapter 2

Face the Fear

You gain strength, courage and confidence by every experience in which you really stop to look fear in the face. . . . You must do the thing you think you cannot do.

—Eleanor Roosevelt

As a child, I was afraid of heights. I would tell people that I was afraid of heights, thinking that my announcement would somehow eliminate any chance of my having to climb anything ever again. The only problem was, I kept finding myself in situations involving the very thing I feared: heights. Yikes!

There were two things I failed to recognize. First, no one really gives a damn if you are scared or not. In my world, you were expected to either find the courage to do it or get the hell out of the way for those who would. Second, we attract what we think of and dwell on. Life has a way of forcing you to face your fears—if you want to reach the good stuff, that is. While it seemed about as far from good as you can get at the time, the stories that follow forced me to face my fear.

When we first began wrestling for the wild drill-sergeant coach, all of the kids who signed up were scared shitless, and for good reason. As brand new nine- and ten-year-old little league wrestlers, we were expected to climb all the way to the top of the thirty-foot rope in the gymnasium—which seemed nuts, since most of the high school athletes couldn't even do it. There were no landing mats either; you'd just better hang on tight.

I remember my first time trying to climb the rope. I made it up maybe halfway and was done. My arms were on fire, and I thought I might fall. All of a sudden, I felt the rope shaking and getting stiff. I looked down and saw the crazed coach with a wooden board clenched between his teeth, climbing like a monkey up the rope toward me. While hanging on with one hand, he then proceeded to beat my legs and ass with the board in his free hand. We were dangling about fifteen feet above the ground, and I was looking down, trying to kick him off of me. I could see the other kids staring up from their seated positions on the gym floor, their eyes wide open in disbelief, taking in the craziness transpiring above their heads, waiting and dreading their turn to make the excruciating climb.

Instead of spurring me to climb higher, the clubbing had just the opposite effect. In a split second, I decided if this nut wanted to hit my scrawny ass with a board, we were going to do it on the ground. At that instant, I let go and all seventy-eight pounds of me collapsed down the rope, using the coach's head and upper body to break my fall, which caused the whole shit show to fall to the ground from about seven feet up. On the way down, that crazed coach was still trying to hit me with that damn board—that is, until we crashed in a pile on the hard gym floor. What an ordeal. I had a few tears and bruises, but, surprisingly, I was okay, since I'd landed on top of the coach. I think he may have been stunned by that fall, because I don't remember him saying much or ever doing that again. Thankfully the bell rang, indicating class was over, and everyone disappeared like the wind.

My next battle with heights occurred around this same age when a buddy and I decided it would be a great idea to sneak down to the local grain elevator, located along the train tracks that ran through our town, and gather up a few pigeons while they were napping up top. Of course, this was after the facility had closed for the evening, which, since it was the middle of winter, meant it was also dark. Not a problem; we had a plan.

The plan was to ride to the top of this enormous high-rise wheat storage building in the tiny, chain-driven, two-man lift that was built into the center of the structure. We would do this in a cloud of wheat dust and darkness, all so we could snatch some pigeons off of their roost while they dreamed of sunflower seeds.

Well, the plan was working out fine. We had our flashlight and pillowcase, and after a few nerve-racking minutes, the rickety old lift carried us to the top. I know what you're thinking: Why in the world? I ask myself that same question now; however, it seemed like a brilliant idea at the time. We finally got to the top of the giant grain elevator and—surprise!—we found no pigeons. *I'm sure they heard the junky old lift and flew off,* I thought to myself. *Oh well, probably for the best,* said the voice of reason in my head.

We moved our attention down to the streetlights scattered across our dimly lit town. Our chests swelled with pride thinking we were standing on top of the world. Then, in a split second, everything changed. Our proud moment was interrupted by the sudden and stinging impact of sleet that began to fall. We were instantly overwhelmed with the realization that it was way too damn wet, cold, and dark, and we needed to get the hell off the top of that gigantic structure—and fast.

At this point, we discovered that the little elevator that had carried us to the top was no longer working. With only a shared look of total disbelief and grave concern, we both knew what this meant: someone was going to have to climb down the flimsy wrought iron ladder that was attached to the concrete exterior. This so-called ladder looked more like a human death trap than an escape route. While it did extend all the way down to the cold, dark ground, of course, we couldn't actually see it at that point. One of us needed to have a sudden burst of courage, and fast, because the sleet was starting to cover everything in a layer of ice. The situation was growing more critical with every passing second.

I'm not sure how it was decided so fast, maybe because my friend outweighed me by twenty pounds or more, but I was the one who had to climb down that rickety old ladder. I remember being terrified for my life as I lay on my stomach and eased my legs over the frozen, slippery edge. With only my torso remaining on the slick structure, I franticly struggled to stretch my worn-out cowboy boots toward the ridiculously low first step. My body began to cramp almost immediately. After what had to be thirty of the most grueling minutes of clinging for my life, thankfully, I finally reached revered Mother Earth.

I was about to go for help to get the lift back on for my buddy up top, when the owner of the grain elevator came driving up. The crazy thing is he had been sitting in his warm office listening to the whole reckless ordeal on his intercom system. *He* was the one who had shut the damn lift off! Looking back, I'm sure he was entertained by my harrowing experience. Honestly, I was not sure I would even make it down. For me, that was it. After that death-defying climb for my life, which turned out to be utterly unnecessary, I never wanted to be above the sacred solid ground again.

Obviously, these experiences, and others, contributed to my fear of heights. I did, however, commit myself to overcoming that fear. It took some time, but I eventually became skilled at climbing the rope as a high school wrestler. Also, over the years, I've taken private pilot training and even gone so far as performing a tandem skydive jump out of a DC-3 at 13,000 feet with the freefall lasting over one minute. I was also able to become somewhat of a rock climber, with a little help from my gym buddy and extreme athlete, Cecil. The summer I turned thirty-two, my friend and I camped and climbed the cliffs of Yosemite Valley. We even climbed base routes on El Capitan—3,000 feet of sheer vertical granite. Looking back on it all, it was hard to believe I was able to experience such an epic adventure, considering how terrified of heights I was as a youth. I had finally turned the fear into courage, thanks to my buddy's encouragement and my own determination.

When it comes to facing your fears, remember that all things are in transition. Try to think in relative terms. Perhaps consider that the oldest living creature on this earth is thought to be a clam, clocking in at around 500 years old. Next is a Greenland shark at 390, a sea urchin at 200, and a Galápagos tortoise at 177 years old. Sorry to say, humans average somewhere between seventy and eighty years based on their region, and that's if all goes well. The point is, soon enough we will all die and eventually turn into a small handful of dust. There's no need to hurry or rush the transition, but also no need to hold back when it comes to chasing your dreams and conquering challenges. For time is short, and youth is even shorter. Learn to face and channel your fears. Imagine the fear, and feel it turning into positive energy as it passes through you.

Another powerful unwritten law of our species is that, when we apply ourselves and really try, we are capable of getting ourselves out of seemingly impossible and unsurvivable situations. We can accomplish these incredible feats because, according to scientists, we have somewhere between 36 and 70 trillion cells in our body, each one producing an electrical impulse that is triggered by the brain. When we focus this energy with belief and conviction on something we know must be done to preserve our very existence (like having to climb down that grain elevator), these cells kick in and begin to move in sync toward that end. This brain-created energy force taps into all of our internal resources in an attempt to overcome and survive whatever we may face. Throughout this book you will read that thoughts have power and energy beyond ourselves. Believe it. Use this force of perspective by first defining and then conquering the appropriate fears and obstacles needed to propel you toward your goals. Tackling your fears actually becomes empowering when approached with the correct mindset. This is when exponential growth can occur.

Life has a way of giving you the very thing you hate, the very thing you fear. At some point we are all going to face criticism, haters, rejection and loss. The best way to avoid being criticized is to sit on your ass and try nothing, say nothing and become nothing. People won't be talking about you then! Realize that you can never please everyone and that most, if not all, folks are wired to question and disagree, no matter what the topic. You can reject, learn from or completely ignore other people's opinions. What you think, the perspective you take, is the only thing that really matters. All the power is with you. Do you ignore this energy, thereby perpetuating a chaotic condition? Or do you use it, shape and mold it to work for you as best you can and then accept the rest as it is?

Mastery of anything can become a certainty with perseverance and discipline. Put less faith in fear and more faith in love and empowerment. Know that you can improve and move forward from any position. Strive for your peak performance in all areas. That's the discipline we should seek, to continue to stretch ourselves, to display control and self-correct when needed, to face the fear head on, and to constantly search for ways to make progress, no matter how small. It won't be easy, especially in the beginning, but by practicing and thinking in these terms, we find that courage can start to become engrained and second nature. To paraphrase "The Duke," courage is being scared to death but saddling up anyway.

While most of us are terrified to get up in front of people to speak or perform, this next story is about a young lady of sixteen who has overcome this all-too-common fear in order to showcase her abilities as a talented singer. Her name is Cora Beth and she has been performing locally since age five, starting with churches and schools, and then on to the Rodeo Opry and the Lyric Theatre of Oklahoma. She has even performed at the Clay Cooper Theatre in Branson, Missouri, and at Disneyland in California.

Most recently, Cora reached her goal of auditioning for *American Idol.* While she did not get a pass to move on to the second round, she caught the attention of one of the judges, who pulled her aside. He told her he was inspired by her performance and her story and felt that she could have a tremendous career. The judge did not want her to be discouraged by the panel's decision, because he saw the potential of this beautiful young woman to have an impact on thousands of lives. He advised Cora Beth to continue on her path of music and performing, but to use her performances to help educate—to bridge the gap and blur the lines between those who have physical and mental challenges and those who don't. You see, when Cora was born, she weighed less than two pounds. As a result, she developed a debilitating brain condition known as cerebral palsy and now requires a walker to get around. Although she has endured unimaginable obstacles, you would never know it to see or talk with her. Her courage seems normal to her, but I assure you, she is a champion like no other.

We can't see the future, but my hunch is that Cora will take the advice of that *American Idol* judge and have a tremendous career that involves inspiring others to find the courage to face their own fears and to find compassion, understanding and goodness within themselves—all the things Cora has been doing in her local community since early childhood. My hope is that this book might spark a desire for Cora Beth to someday write about her long and remarkable journey. Hammer down, sister!

ħ

Chapter 3

Find Your Truth

The willingness to empty ourselves and then seek our true nature is an expression of great and courageous love.

—Jack Kornfield

When I think of finding balance and being grounded in truth, I am reminded that so often these things are discovered through great loss and much sacrifice. This certainly seems to be the case for my friend Joe, who is an Oklahoma City firefighter. Joe has been on the job for twenty-five years, which means he has seen some horrible things. On April 19, 1995, as a rookie with only six months on the job, he was one of the first responders to the bombing of the Alfred P. Murrah Federal Building. This cowardly act of terrorism claimed the lives of 168 people, including nineteen children under the age of six. Mere moments after the explosion, the sirens rang out across our city. As some of the first few to arrive on scene, Joe and his comrades desperately tried to attend to the overwhelming number of injured and walking wounded, while others were frantically digging and searching through the smoldering rubble for survivors. Most of the responders worked to the point of total exhaustion. With half of the building destroyed, and with fire and smoke still billowing from the carnage, the scene quickly turned from one of rescue to one of recovery.

Joe and I met and became friends in 2004, nine years after this terrible act was committed against our community. Around this same time, disaster struck Joe's family when one of his younger brothers, Mike, was killed in a tragic auto collision. Only eighteen months later, Matt, twin brother of Mike, died in a freak four-wheeler accident. To say that Joe's family has experienced its share of loss and tragedy is quite the understatement; yet they, like many others, endure and press onward.

When I consider the trauma, heartache, death, and utterly detestable things that Joe has seen and endured over his long career as a firefighter, it is truly mind-boggling. I share all this with you because when I think of the most spiritually grounded and balanced person I know, I think of my friend Joe. Not because he is without fault—he's not—but because of his grace and the way he is a cornerstone for his family and friends, and because of the way that he and many others in uniform shield and protect us from the ugliness and heartache that continue to occur in our society.

Over the years I have had many a good conversation around the campfire with my old fishing buddy, and after more than a decade, I am still affected by the quiet calm he exudes. Our conversations usually cover almost anything, from our kids to hunting and fishing, horses and wrestling, and even our faith. But on occasion we talk about how he deals with all the images of trauma and death he has seen throughout his long career.

He explained his pragmatic approach to me like this: Someone has to run toward the problem, so why not him? "That's my job and why I am here." He also strives to be grounded in his faith and belief in God, and he credits the strong support system he has in his loving family and close friends.

You would think a person would become bitter and jaded in his type of work. To the contrary, it is a rare encounter that I am not lifted in spirit when Joe and I meet up. Our open and honest conversation is truly therapeutic, not to mention it helped inspire the creation of this book. Joe is exactly the kind of person I want to be associated with and am proud to call a friend. He knows who he is. He is grounded in his faith and values, and, in his words, "The demons are always there, but I keep getting a little stronger with each passing day!" You might say Joe knows how to live.

Seek Spiritual Energy

We are not human beings having a spiritual experience.

We are spiritual beings having a human experience.

—Pierre Teilhard de Chardin (attributed)

Spiritual power is a difficult thing to understand and explain to someone who has not felt it. It must be experienced and felt in your heart and soul in order to know it. Imagine for a moment a person who has never had sugar. You can describe it to them in detail, explain how it is made, and even let them reach down and grab a handful of it, but until they taste the sugar, they can never truly know what it is. Spiritual matters are much the same.

When I wish to feel more spiritually balanced, I begin with the simple thought that all living things are connected. In fact, advances in modern science have enabled experts to determine that particles found in the human body are also detected in space rocks. This leaves us with one conclusion: We are all made of star dust! That is, we are all connected to *everything*. I imagine that was an "aha" moment for the team of researchers and scientists.

There are over eight million species on this planet. The incredible abundance of life we get to enjoy is breathtaking, if you happen to notice it. Most people get so caught up in their daily routines and habits of living for tomorrow that they forget to notice the real story and the real show. Look up to the night sky, take in the vastness of it all, and realize that everything you see is ever-changing and connected—everything, including you. Stop for a moment and consider how much life is outside your front door—plants, animals, birds, insects, trees, grass, people—life and love are everywhere. Even the air itself feels alive. You need only to have yourself in the proper frame of mind to see and receive the energy through you. Become one of the parts needed to make the whole of life itself at this very moment in time. Know it as fact that you are part of the whole.

The realization that all living things have the same creator, that all living things are connected, is the state of mind that we should try to develop and feel. It is a deep and certain feeling, the same way we know that one plus one equals two. We would never think to argue otherwise or find it necessary to defend this fact; it just is. Know and feel your connectedness to the universe in the same way, and you will begin to develop spiritual balance.

I believe, as many others do, that my God is one of life-giving forces—wisdom, love and forgiveness—whose energy is available to those conscious enough to notice and become part of it. I also believe that the Creator made all of us in his image, which means there is a piece of God buried deep within each of us. This incredible energy seems to be locked in our subconscious mind, which has been described as a vast ocean compared to our conscious mind. The conscious mind represents a giant container ship on this ocean—still big, but nothing compared to the subconscious. We have the ability to move into the subconscious ocean of the mind and access its power if we can quiet the ego.

It is a scientific fact that what we think in our mind creates and sends out a rhythm of electrical vibrations and frequencies. These subtle but powerful thoughts and impulses engage the law of attraction, which then works to attract and manifest what the mind thinks (so it would be wise to make it good!).

Throughout the universe, things seem to operate on a cycle or in a rhythm. We know when the moon will eclipse the sun, when the seasons will turn and snow will fall, the twenty-four-hour cycle of day and night, and even the rhythm of our own breathing and heartbeat. If we can slow down and be present enough to line up with the frequencies and vibrations of nature and even the universe, great power can be accessed. Great minds from our past, like da Vinci, Einstein, Jobs and Tesla, all spoke of getting their ideas and inspiration from a higher power, from "space." It appears they may have developed the ability to tap into this remarkable force.

When considering the immense power of unseen forces, from those throughout the universe to those within our own bodies, we should also realize that most of us tend to focus solely on what we can see and touch. Unfortunately, a tremendous amount is missed when this occurs. The real power and energy is found in the unseen forces.

Consider for a moment the grasses that spread across the Great Plains of the American West. Many people will be surprised to learn that a variety called buffalo grass, *Buchloe dactyloides*, grows only to a height of four to six inches. The remarkable thing about this resilient prairie grass is that its roots plunge into the earth at a depth of up to eight feet. That's around twenty times more going on below ground than what we see happening above ground. Some varieties of prairie grass roots will grow over fifteen feet into the earth. This is the power and energy of unseen forces in their most basic and revealing form.

I am no scientist, doctor, or for that matter, watchmaker. I cannot explain all of the technical and intricate workings of a watch's gears and springs or why it works like it does—nor do I need to. I only need to be able to slow down and see the time. The time is now, of course, as it always is. Again, I make no claims of having or finding all the answers. In fact, quite the contrary. Much of what I have learned has been through my many years of doing things wrong, as so often seems to be the case. After a few decades of trial and error, I've come to realize that if we wish to tap into the universal forces that are available to us all, we first must move our mind and soul to "open and receive" mode. This then allows a portal of entry for spiritual energy.

Become conscious and mindful of what you think, say and do. The vibrations you put off are what you become. Begin to think in terms of balance and being connected to nature. Then, when the ego wants to take over, tap into this feeling of knowing and connection. While the ego does have a place and is not necessarily a bad thing, it is reckless and inefficient in that it allows excessive loss of precious energy and internal resources. If you want to have spiritual balance and access the power of the unseen forces, whether through praying in church on Sunday or meditating on Monday, the ego should be muted and moved to the side. We must keep the message we send to ourselves positive and good if that is how we wish to feel. This is the reason I meditate and pray daily—to search for and feel spiritual balance within.

I have included in this chapter some of the practical techniques that I have found useful when I wish to slow the mind and search within.

Feel Sincere Appreciation

If you aren't grateful for what you already have, what makes you think you would be happy with more?

—Roy T. Bennett

It may sound like a cliché, but one of the most important lessons I have learned is this: do not take things for granted. In fact, I encourage you to do just the opposite: practice gratitude. How grateful are you that you are able to breathe in fresh clean air, enjoy a glass of cool water, or hear the sound of children laughing? Each morning take time to appreciate what you already have. At the beginning of each day, write down three things you are thankful for. You will start to see and feel changes within the month. In one year, you will be forever changed.

This is the solid foundation from which we want to build. Regardless of your faith or spiritual practice, starting your day off by being mindful and grateful for the blessings you have now will help move you to a receptive frame of mind. Establishing a daily routine of deep appreciation allows your mind to shift from closed to open, where positive forces can then begin to move through you. Operating with a grateful disposition begins to activate the unseen energy. Again, you must move your ego out of the way, and remember that true power comes from within.

Begin each day with this practice and watch this simple but effective shift transform you.

Learn to illuminate and cherish each moment as it passes. Quietly savor life. Stop blindly blowing past it in a frenzy to get to the future.

Seek Connection

We are like islands in the sea, separate on the surface
but connected in the deep.
—William James (attributed)

There seems to be no limit to the insane risks and wild extremes people will endure in order to feel alive and connected to something bigger. We are the only species, it seems, that will intentionally seek out intensely painful, terrifying, even life-threatening situations in order to experience exhilaration and joy, if only for a brief moment.

We should all try to find and create circumstances that will leave us feeling empowered and connected, but in no way do I believe they have to be life-threatening. Finding connection can come in many forms. Even activities as simple as walking in nature, volunteering, or listening to a particular kind of music all carry the potential for connection.

When our Grampa Andy was in his late eighties, my brothers Randy and Tim and I took Gramp, as we called him, to his family reunion in Magdalena, New Mexico. This rough but beautiful country is where he grew up, cowboying and scratching out a living.

I remember one evening, as the sun was setting in spectacular fashion, the few scattered clouds were brilliantly illuminated in the most intense palette of orange, red and purple hues against a vibrant blue background. The final few minutes of sunlight painted the rugged but colorful valley grasses below as we watched in awe from a small outcrop of pinion pine trees where the family had gathered. My brother Randy and I decided it would be a great time to hike up the rocky pinion covered hill and get a better view of what can only be described as the most glorious sunset we had ever witnessed. While sitting there taking in this entrancing landscape, we began to hear the sounds of beautiful hymns being sung by our Spanish relatives from the pavilion below. I will never forget those few precious moments on that hill. As the songs of what sounded like Spanish angels echoed in the soft breeze, my brother and I slowly turned to each other with a mesmerized look of absolute joy merged with complete silence, so as to take in the incredible experience unfolding before us. Not a word was spoken or a sound made by either of us for what seemed an hour or more as we both tried to savor these glorious and fleeting final few moments. Reflecting back on this precious memory left me with the sense that we were truly in the presence of God that evening. I will never forget the incredible feeling that captivating sunset awakened within me. This type of connected-to-nature experience inspired me to write a little poem a few years back.

SOUNDS OF EVENING

The sounds of evening just before dark,
across the lake I hear the meadow lark,
the coyote howls and the multitude join in,
the birds now nesting as another day ends.
For just a few moments they all seem to stir.
I feel I can hear each and every bird.
The spirit begins to listen as the mind tries to see;
it becomes only sounds as my soul is set free.
All seem to bid farewell as their songs echo in the eve.
It is this time of the day, that I thank God I believe.
The critters of the day all seem to nestle in.

In a sudden moment the stillness of night begins.
My eyes drift toward the stars and my soul awakens.
In the blink of an eye I'm traveling through the
heavens.
Nature's daily miracle is for all to see;
you only have to open your heart to the sounds, the sky,
and the breeze.
Humbled by the rhythm of day turning to night,
to pray now only seems right.

Find the things that leave you feeling empowered and connected. Look for similarities and feel the connectedness in all things. This approach and perspective will help keep you in an open and receptive state of mind.

Serve Others

For even the Son of Man did not come to be served,
but to serve, and to give his life as a ransom for many.
—Mark 10:45 (NIV)

The giving of one's self is an excellent way to continue to operate and exist in a positive and receptive state. Hopefully we can all know the good feeling that comes from donating to a local shelter, or regularly contributing to churches and other worthy charities and causes. These are certainly generous and noble acts of good character. However, the giving of one's own time and self to others, with no expectation of reciprocity, seems to set in play subtle yet powerful forces that otherwise lie dormant. The forces that can be awakened through the giving of your time have the potential to turn you into an instrument for good, an extension of God himself in your act of serving others.

My older brother Rick recently retired after working twenty-three years at a federal prison. He even flew "Con Air" (prisoner transportation) for a time. Since Rick enjoys various hobbies like trading cattle, training horses, riding motorcycles, working on his monster truck, deer hunting, camping, fishing and boating, playing guitars, and playing golf—not to mention spending time with his grandkids and helping out his family and friends—he is a busy guy. Yet he still decides to drive down to the local Mobile Meals kitchen and volunteer to deliver meals to the elderly and those unable to prepare their own food. Each week for two years, my brother would make his rounds by bringing hot food to the front doors of the grateful folks on his route.

I took the opportunity to join my brother a few times and even ran his route once when he was out on vacation. We'll always remember the last stop of the day, a kind and cheerful elderly lady named Miss Edna who reminded us of our cherished Grandma Haley from our youth—complete with lilac bush, screen door, and a smile that always refueled the heart. It was obvious that she greatly looked forward to my brother's brief visits, and I could see the feeling was mutual. After two years of weekly stops, the day came when Rick noticed her name was no longer on his list of recipients. Realizing that she was very likely all alone, we were both saddened to hear of Miss Edna's passing.

To say that you gain much more than you give when you serve others seems to very often, if not always, be the case. Had we not donated a little time to serve others with the Mobile Meals, we would have never had the chance to meet the kind and cheerful lady who reminded us so much of our beloved Grandma Haley.

Would you like to feel good about yourself? Go spend time and help someone less fortunate. If you've reached your goals, don't forget to reach back; be a mentor and lift up someone else who may not have a chance otherwise.

Meditate and Pray

Prayer is not an old woman's idle amusement.
Properly understood and applied, it is the most
potent instrument of action.
—Mahatma Gandhi

Daily prayer and meditative practices seem to allow access to the subconscious regions of the mind. Even today there are those who spend their entire lives in deep meditation, searching for and dwelling in this state of mindfulness and prayer. But meditation is not some kind of mysterious and unattainable tool reserved only for the enlightened. You and I can access the same forces; we only have to condition ourselves. The benefits are available to anyone with the wisdom to search.

If there is a magic pill for an improved mindset, daily meditation is it. The portals that open when you are in deep meditation can have tremendous benefits on your state of mind and on your life as a whole. By learning to operate from within, to be present in every moment with all your focus placed on the "right now," you then exist in a state of balance and harmony with all things that are happening right now, which is everything.

As you aim to direct your focus inward, remember it is not *about* you but *through* you. Meditation is not a practice used to gain something material. It is the redirecting of our attention to the unseen—above, below and within. It is the calming and tuning of one's frequencies, rhythms and vibrations to be in harmony with those of nature and the universe. It is not something that is worked for or attained, but rather something that is felt by allowing the peaceful practice itself to be moving and liberating.

There are a variety of meditation methods one can learn and experience. Most have heard of or seen the calm and quiet sitting technique; there is also walking meditation. In some methods you chant different sounds; in others, you concentrate on a single candle flame or a dot on an imaginary piece of paper. Regardless of the technique, when you are able to quiet the internal dialogue that goes on in your mind, you can then move into a receptive state. This is when positive energy will begin to work through you. Meditation is kind of like getting out of your own way. Correction: it is *exactly* like getting out of your own way.

At the risk of offending at least a few different religions, I will say that prayer and meditation are much the same to me. Through meditation, my prayer becomes more meaningful. As mentioned previously, spiritual energies are difficult to understand and explain; they must be felt. While I too have distracting thoughts and difficulty concentrating at times, here is how I go about tapping into and feeling those forces, and I recommend you try it as well.

Position and posture. I begin by finding a quiet place. For me, it's normally my living room, but out in nature is great, too. I usually sit on my sports ball—but you can sit on the ground or on a chair—with good posture, my nose just slightly above level. (When I catch myself dropping below level, I simply adjust back to the proper position and continue.) I open my hands, palms up, and rest them comfortably on my knees.

The breath. I begin by taking a few slow, deep breaths in and out through my nose; then I gently close my eyes, relax, and breathe normally. As I slowly and calmly breathe in and out, I focus on the feeling of each breath. My mind follows each breath as it moves from the tip of my nose, into my head, and then down into my chest and abdominal area. I envision myself breathing in the most precious and powerful life-giving energy and expelling any remaining stress, negativity, or self-doubt with each exhale as it passes out through my nose.

Often I imagine—actually it's more of a feeling—that Jesus is praying and meditating with me. I sense him sitting across from me; his hands are in mine and we are breathing the same holy air, although in my imagination it is more like radiant light.

The inhale. With each inhale I try to vividly imagine a ribbon of pure, intense white light. I imagine that this powerful, sun-like glow illuminates and vitalizes every dark corner of my internal system, from head to toe. I try to follow and feel each breath all the way down into the abdominal area, where the imagined intense light is deposited and then absorbed. This internal brilliance then dissolves any impurities or unhealthy messages throughout my body.

The exhale. The exhale begins and ends with a puff of imagined carbon dust particles from the release, which represents the expulsion of any negativity, stress or weakness in my body. All of the light and positive life-giving energy remains within, at my center.

I know it sounds heavy, and of course most people will fail to even try, but this is all done in an instant and with each and every breath. The simple act of breathing in and out can be quite invigorating when you begin to turn your focus inward to the unseen world.

Again, there are many ways to meditate and pray; there is no right or wrong way. And don't worry if you are easily distracted; simply return your attention back to your breath. This is the actual practice of meditation: learning to identify and move away from the distraction and back to within. This shift of focus back to the unseen is when you are flexing and working on your meditation muscle, the brain.

After you gain more experience with the breathing method of focus in meditation, you will be able to catch yourself complaining or having negative thoughts and quietly shift your attention back to your breathing in order to evaporate these self-defeating conditions, all on the fly. You are now gaining control over your internal dialogue. This is a liberating and empowering feeling.

If you want peace in your life, if you want to be truly happy, you must attend to and nourish your spirit. Whether through religious services, personal prayer, meditation, or time spent in nature, establish a daily routine that involves awakening, nourishing and developing your spirit.

Hopefully, we will never have to experience a fraction of the horrible things that my buddy Joe and our nation's first responders have to endure on a regular basis. However, by nurturing and developing your spiritual balance on a daily basis, you then develop a path to peace and gain the capacity to handle whatever life throws your way the very best you can.

ℏ

Chapter 4

Manage Your Mind

The evil that afflicts us is not external, it is within us . . . [F]or that reason we attain soundness with all the more difficulty, because we do not know that we are diseased.

—Seneca the Younger

Perhaps you have heard the story of the old Cherokee Brave who was counseling his grandson on the meaning of life. "Inside of me, there is a great battle that rages between two wolves," he said. "The first wolf is evil and represents hate, anger, greed, envy, guilt, sorrow, self-pity and ego." The old grandfather continued, "The second wolf is good and stands for hope, joy, benevolence, courage, kindness, love and faith. This battle rages within us all." After thinking about what his grandfather had said for a moment, the young boy looked up and asked, "But which wolf will win?" The grandfather replied simply, "The one you feed."

This parable describes the silent struggle going on within each of us. It also points out that the "wolf" that shows up is the one that gets nurtured and receives your attention. People can never be perfect, of course; life is a mixture of good and evil, and that first wolf representing our ego is always going to be there fighting for survival. The goal is to find a balance, or harmony if you will. Make sure you are making room for and feeding the right wolf.

Without a doubt, the most important thing I will write within these pages is the importance of having a positive mental attitude and keeping good, empowering thoughts flowing in your brain. If you want to be happier and find peace, you must first understand the mind's tendency to wander into self-criticism and self-defeating thinking, and then learn ways to control and reverse these negative patterns. Over a person's lifetime there will be many attacks on the spirit and the ego. We will get our feelings hurt over and over again throughout the years, then as we replay the scenarios over and over in our head, those hurt feelings can fester and turn into anger, or worse. These memories are very powerful because of the emotion and passion associated with them. They get stored and layered on top of one another until we've built such a wall of negativity and defensiveness that it becomes hard to see how we can ever become the healthy, happy person we were truly meant to be—one without all the excess baggage and self-imposed limitations. It is amazing the speed and accuracy our egos have in accessing, exaggerating and repeatedly reliving these powerful negative memories and emotions.

The seemingly magical power of our brain is perception, and we can control that with focus. We can slingshot and use those same forces in a positive direction. All the walls we've built over the years can be vaporized in an instant with the proper mindset. Perhaps you will recall the scene from the movie *Braveheart* where Robert the Bruce betrayed William Wallace in his critical time of need. Robert had given his word, but then listened to the evil lies of treachery and compromise from his diseased father. Robert's father convinced him the same way the bad wolf is always trying to convince us. He would later say to him, "All men betray; all men lose heart."

Torn apart from his betrayal, in tears of anger, Robert sternly shouted back, "I don't want to lose heart! I want to believe as he [Wallace] does. . . I will never be on the wrong side again." At that instant Robert the Bruce's life altered course. He broke his word, then saw and felt the consequences of it. It crushed him. Robert vowed then and there to never again compromise his values.

Begin by finding out who you are and become firmly grounded in that. For some, it may help to first point out and clearly identify what you are *not*, what you refuse to become. Undependable, lazy, a cheat, a drunk, and a coward are but a few examples from my list. Once you clearly document what you *refuse* to become, you can then begin to recognize and document the things that give you energy and move you toward the principles you value. Become a beacon of positive energy for your family, your faith, and your friends, but more importantly for yourself. The practice of offering daily gratitude and tuning into nature's vibrations and energy can be your catalyst.

Once you get a firm understanding of who you are, never partake in any activity that threatens or goes against your values or peace of mind. Ever. Good character is a precious thing to have and hard to get back once lost. Best to guard this and your spirit from all life- and energy-draining sources. Seemingly every important situation comes with a choice, a path that must be taken. There are many turns and trails that will tempt us, but these are not the right path. The right path is one of honesty, virtue and grit. Deep within our heart we know which path seems most right; seek and choose that one.

After a tragic accident and discovering firsthand the power that our mind and thoughts have over our health and healing, a man by the name of Phil Parker developed a medical treatment program that deals with the neuroplasticity of the brain and the brain's impact on treating illnesses. Within his program, he discusses the findings of FDA placebo drug trials and the dramatic results that can occur within patients who believe they are taking medicine. In one such case, 40 percent of the group who received the placebo drug lost all bodily hair due to the fact they believed they were receiving chemo treatments. The "chemo drugs" were sugar pills. Once your belief becomes conviction, once you know it to be true, great and strange results can and will occur.

Additionally, according to molecular biologist and neuroscientist Bruce H. Lipton, despite the billions of dollars spent on the anti-depressant Prozac each year, this drug has been found to be no more effective than a placebo. Yet people spend their money on Prozac, thinking it is helping them, when it is, in fact, their *belief* in the pill that helps them. Lipton goes on to say that studies have also shown that up to one-third of all healing, including surgery, is a result of the placebo effect. That is, the patient gets better solely from the belief that the doctor did something to make them better. The power of belief can and does produce miraculous outcomes.

Someone once said if you knew the power of your thoughts, you would never have another negative one. It is estimated that we have as many as 60,000 thoughts each and every day. If you learn to dissolve even one negative thought—or, better yet, turn it into a positive and empowering thought—you can develop the power to change everything.

Doctor Lipton went on to reveal that, on average, 95 percent of our daily tasks are performed not by the conscious mind as one would hope, but by our subconscious, or auto pilot if you will. If you are performing a task like walking or driving and you are thinking of anything other than walking or driving, your subconscious is in control.

The trick is to get the wishes and desires of your conscious mind to line up with the same wishes and desires in your subconscious. This way, whether the conscious or subconscious mind is activated, you're still seeking and playing the same wishes and desires loop. Not that easy to do at first but it can be done. This is when seemingly magical forces can begin to materialize.

If our minds have this kind of power, let us firmly know it and then own it. Realize we can learn methods, techniques and even tricks to harness this energy to work for us in a positive fashion. Over these many years, in my own quest for growth, fused with a deep curiosity and hunger for wisdom, I have read many authors and applied a variety of practices. This includes books on leadership, personal development and pursuing your goals, mostly because I am curious about the effectiveness of each method. While many of these seemingly modern techniques appear new and revolutionary, most stem from ancient teachings.

Fifteen years ago, after having lunch at a local Chinese restaurant, I strolled out with fortune cookie in hand. Since this restaurant had been my go-to spot for a couple of years at this point, I had read and nibbled on enough fortune cookies from this place to feed a buffalo. My usual routine was to toss the stale token in the provided gum-splattered trash can. However, that day, for some reason, I decided to chew the wrapper open and see what words of wisdom lay inside. Even these many years later I have to say I was not disappointed. The simple, and yet profound, message I walked away with was not insignificant. The paper slip included a phrase that originated over five thousand years ago. The simple words read: "Before enlightenment, chop wood, carry water. After enlightenment, chop wood, carry water." The lesson I took away from these words is that our journey does not end when we reach our goals. We must continue to strive for understanding, growth and wisdom.

I was not sure why it resonated with me so much at the time, but I now understand that these few words of wisdom helped me expand my understanding that everything worthwhile is a process: success, growth, healing, even love. I don't take away from this that life will always be a struggle, although I realize that for multitudes it is. At some point, everyone will face tragedy, hardship and suffering. The meaning of this simple lesson to me is this: if you find something worthwhile to you, do your best to work toward that end and keep doing that until the end. Find your purpose and stay with it.

The tender ends of a tree's root system plunge deeply and effortlessly into the hard earth and rock, not through struggle and intensity, but through continual pressure and persistency. Do your best and continue to do so. This is a maxim I myself embrace each day.

Seek Discomfort

Be not afraid of discomfort. If you can't put yourself in a situation where you are uncomfortable, then you will never grow. You will never change. You'll never learn.
—Jason Reynolds

It is no secret that we as humans prefer structure and routine. The problems start when our structure and routines are destructive to ourselves and others. We all subconsciously seek out answers to reinforce what we already believe, even if what we believe is wrong. And we do this without even being aware of it. We argue and defend our position as if we know what is true and correct. More often than not our beliefs are based on what we've heard or read someone else say or write, which is seen through their filter and their bias of the world. Our egos fool us. We believe we are happy and comfortable in our current state, but many times it is that exact thing keeping us from living a bigger, more fulfilling, and purposeful existence.

It makes perfect sense to want to take the path of least resistance, to stay in our comfort zone, to avoid any type of failure. In fact, this is the approach most people take; unfortunately, most will never even get close to reaching their full potential. However, there are those who recognize that growth cannot take place in a soft and unchallenging environment. For growth to take place, we must be willing to take risks—risk of failure and risk of being hurt, criticized or ridiculed by others. We must be honest with ourselves and learn to be vulnerable if we want to experience the good things life has to offer. We must remove the barriers and walls that we accumulate over the years and expose our soft underbelly. This is where the truth dwells.

If we continue to defend and protect our feelings from the fear of failure or judgment, we will never get what we want. It is true that the judgment of others can have a paralyzing effect on us, if we allow it, and we may very well fail in our efforts. But when we have a setback, it is important to frame the experience as a learning and growth opportunity. We should simply adjust our approach and try again.

Create an environment that requires you to push through the things that make you a little uncomfortable, the things that stretch you. Once again this is where you will become stronger and wiser. Put yourself in situations that, when you do succeed, leave you feeling empowered and fulfilled.

Quiet the Anger

Holding onto anger is like drinking poison and expecting the other person to die.

—Anonymous

While having passion is a good thing, it can often turn into anger and bitterness, which, once started, tend to become exaggerated and build on themselves. There is a time and place for anger. There is no question it can be quite the motivator when called upon. However, holding onto these adverse emotions has been scientifically proven to have a negative impact on your well-being and overall performance. Self-correct using the breathing and mindfulness techniques discussed earlier:

1. When external events or your own ego begin to cause your thoughts to gravitate toward anger, self-pity or negativity, STOP. Catch yourself, then shift. The moment you realize you are not present, you are present.
2. Take two or three slow, deep breaths through your nose and divert your mind back to the feelings and function of the internal system and your breathing. Simply focus on each breath moving in and out of your body as you breathe normally.
3. Do not battle with your thoughts. View your anger and negativity from afar, with curiosity and an understanding of what lessons may be learned. There's no need to scoop out all the darkness. Just expose it to the light. Then let the negative condition evaporate with your breathing as you embrace the new perspective.
4. The moment you are able to shift your focus back to within, the defeating messages begin to lose their power. All anger and self-defeating thoughts

should be recognized for what they are—the ego fighting for attention.

5. Then move calmly and kindly back to a positive and empowered state, where you belong.

This technique can be mastered and used by anyone, first by understanding that you carry this power over your thoughts, and then with a little practice. Stop letting your mind and the daily external events you experience rob your spirit of precious energy. This space should be reserved for only positive life-giving forces.

The more you perform the simple practice of bringing focus back to the breath, the better you will become at recognizing when the shift is needed. Then, instead of being a slave to your emotions and thoughts, you can learn to turn down the anger and the noise, if only for a few moments at first.

Visualize and Actualize

Visualization and belief in a pattern of reality
activates the creative power of realization.
—A. L. Linall, Jr.

In his groundbreaking book *Psycho-Cybernetics,* Dr. Maxwell Maltz discussed the conditions created by our self-image and the power that thoughts of ourselves carry. Maltz was one of the first to discuss visualization techniques, or "theater of the mind," as he called it: the act of imagining and pretending you already have that which you seek. Maltz, a plastic surgeon by trade, described many documented cases of two similar people having the exact same injury and, because of their mental attitude, experiencing dramatically different recovery outcomes. A scar on the face of one person was worn as a badge of courage, where the same scar on another caused that person to withdraw and feel damaged. Dr. Maltz established visualization techniques to help his patients control how and what they thought with regard to their self-image.

Research has shown these "act as if" visualization methods to be extremely effective at producing results. In many cases, mental practice can be just as effective as physical practice. Years of scientific studies have shown that mental practice will produce the same neuron connections in our brain as actual physical practice. That is, we can physically learn and improve on a skill simply by thinking about it. Of course, combining mental and physical practices is even better.

Consider the professional athletes of today, many of whom use visualization techniques. Watch the elite professionals on the PGA Tour before they step up to hit their shot. Pros like Jason Day and Rickie Fowler visualize the successful execution of the shot and the desired outcome before ever moving into position for the actual shot. At this point, conscious thinking stops; their autopilot kicks in and executes the shot. These visualization methods activate the law of attraction. Remember, we attract what we think about. If we can think it, then see it, and then take it a step further and actually *feel* the sensations associated with these thoughts, we can then develop the ability to reproduce these images and sensations over and over. This is when great and powerful forces can be summoned.

Sort Fact from Opinion

Get your facts first, and then you can distort 'em as much as you please.

—Mark Twain

Dr. Maltz also discussed our mind's tendency to view opinions as facts. For example, someone may say to you, "You are too short; you could never play competitive basketball." It could be a *fact* that you are short, but it is only their *opinion* that you can't play basketball. Try telling Isaiah Thomas, five-foot-nine-inch point guard for the Washington Wizards, that he is too short to play professionally. He excels in a highly competitive game of giants because of his determination and because he believes in himself and his talents.

The thoughts you keep with regard to yourself are of critical importance when it comes to your mood, your health and your ability to perform at a high level. Other people's opinions, of which there will be many, should be seen for what they are: a frequent, and often subconscious, attempt to make them feel better about themselves and their own situation.

Let's face it: the facts do matter. But learn to identify and separate the facts from the opinions. Remember, the only opinion of you that really counts is your own. Develop the art of dealing in facts. Seek out the opinions you value and vaporize the rest.

Accept Feedback

Feedback is the breakfast of champions.

—Rick Tate

Everything is feedback, even the rejected points of view. Every piece of information, every opinion, every failure, every success—everything is feedback to be entered into your mental picture of the world.

Rather than reacting negatively to feedback, accept it. Ask for it. Listen to others with curiosity and the goal of understanding what they have to say, whatever they may offer. Where one person might see randomness, another may see developing patterns. Don't hold to your singular perspective; be open to a new point of view. Be genuine in your curiosity, not by incessant questioning or feigning concern, but by thoughtful attention and a kind, sincere interest.

Realize that with every situation, every encounter, you will always have an opportunity to learn and gain understanding. You only need to look closely enough and have the desire and ability to shift your ego out of the way in order to receive the messages. When it comes to feedback, your ego is not your amigo.

Shift Your Perspective

You have the power over your mind—not outside events.
Realize this and you will find strength.
—Marcus Aurelius

Another method I find useful when I need to get out of my own head is a simple but effective technique revealed in the book *The Power of Now* by Eckhart Tolle. I imagine a mini-me sitting on my shoulder, looking up at me and waiting for my next thought. I move my perspective to that miniature version of me and then I calmly look up at myself and watch and wait. I find this technique to be an extremely effective way to shift my inner dialogue and move back to the present.

When you find that the voice in your head needs quieting or shifting, try this exercise. Say to yourself, from your smaller version sitting on your shoulder, *I wonder what my next thought will be.* Then wait, like a cat watching a mousehole. The moment you do this, the negative thoughts lose their power and you get out of your own head, even if only for a few moments. With practice, this technique becomes more powerful and effortless, and the benefits are tremendous. Become the silent watcher of your mind, the quiet observer.

Consider the Worst Case

If you train worst-case scenarios consistently,
they will no longer be worst-case scenarios.
—Rener Gracie

When I am facing major obstacles and extreme difficulty in life, I use the following process, which allows me to see the issue and keep it front and center. It also helps keep my mind engaged, which then begins to develop potential solutions.

1. Define the problem clearly. Write it down so you can see the issue.
2. Accept that the situation is what it is. Own it. Dive into it with laser focus.
3. Define the worst-case scenario and accept that it could happen. Death perhaps is the worst, so okay, start from there. If death is the worst and I'm still alive, there is a chance the worst won't happen.
4. Document four or five steps you can take to minimize or eliminate the likelihood of the worst-case scenario occurring.
5. Take determined action on those steps. Make taking small steps a huge priority. Improve from where you are right now, wherever that may be. I call this the "no-quit zone." Never give up or stop trying!
6. Whatever the outcome, know that you are doing all you can. Release any fear and worry, and accept what is.

When using this process, you may find your worry and fears have been exaggerated or are even completely unfounded. And if not, at least you are taking action on the issue, which is all you can do. I have no doubt that this process has helped solve some of the world's biggest problems. Do not underestimate its potential to show you the answers you seek.

The ability to let life happen, and the realization that the only thing you can control is *you*, is a liberating state of mind. Work on and develop *that*. As the Buddha put it, it's great if you want to go out and change the world, but first do the harder thing: start by changing yourself.

Live above the Line

When you're finished changing, you're finished.

—Benjamin Franklin (attributed)

One of the most important things we can all learn is that we still have a lot left to learn. In the book *The 15 Commitments of Conscious Leadership*, the authors use a simple horizontal line on an otherwise blank sheet of paper. The space above the line represents consciousness. The space below the line represents unconsciousness. They then ask the question: Are you operating above the line in a positive conscious state, or below the line in a less desirable mode? Meaning, if we live our life below the line, we allow our egos to control our thoughts and actions. We become defensive and closed off. This is when negative forces can take hold of us. But when we operate above the line, we position our minds in an open and receptive state. To truly live above the line is to allow yourself to learn and grow from every experience. So ask yourself: are you operating above the line, or below it?

We all fluctuate above and below this hypothetical line. The goal should not be to spend our entire lives living above the line; that's simply unrealistic. Our goal, instead, should be to let negative thoughts or emotions trigger us to shift back to above-the-line living, to self-correct in order to increase the time spent in the positive state and to limit the below-the-line condition. Our computer—our brain—is constantly searching and browsing through its content. We have the ability to direct this search toward a positive and empowering state. The objective is to recognize when we are in the negative space below the line, and then make the subtle shift above and onward. The imagined line gives you a path back to empowered and positive living. Learn to be self-aware and then to self-regulate when you catch yourself having undesirable thoughts and emotions.

Be determined in your quest for growth, wisdom and even love. The best way to show you really do care about yourself is to have self-discipline. This is how we nurture and feed the good wolf within. Developing the right daily routine is everything.

ħ

Chapter 5

Maintain Your "Vehicle"

One of the greatest moments in life is realizing that two weeks ago your body couldn't do what it just did.

—Anonymous

One summer day, as I was writing this book, my buddy Larry came rolling up in a brand new, jet black, 2019 Tesla Model 3. The second he climbed out of his fancy new rig he began to explain some of the amazing features of this highly sophisticated piece of equipment. From touch-screen controls to an app that allows you to control the car from your smartphone, it is a technical marvel. Equipped with several autopilot features, it can park itself, drive itself down the road with minor driver assistance, and even do a dance across the parking lot.

All day long my buddy bounces around town in his slick new car doing his thing. At night, however, Larry plugs his car in so it can charge. In case you haven't heard, these cars are completely electric and are 100 percent battery-operated.

Checking out my friend's fancy new car reminded me that our bodies are highly sophisticated machines—much more so than even the latest Tesla. Our bodies must be used, or exercised, and then recharged and maintained in the form of sleep and nutrition. Our batteries consist of a delicate balance of food, water and air. If one of these gets out of balance, the situation quickly becomes critical.

Of course, we all know if you want to look and feel your best, the health and condition of your physical body is critically important. Diet, sleep patterns, exercise levels—all your good and destructive habits play a role. Partying every other day like it's the Fourth of July weekend, poor eating habits, and other forms of excess can and will have an adverse impact on your overall health. How healthy your habits and routines are will determine how good you look and feel. It's that simple. This is exactly why we should make our routines and habits exceptional ones. Try it out for yourself; give the difference a test drive. Don't you deserve to be cruising around at your peak performance, feeling your very best?

You don't have to be a doctor or scientist to notice when your body is not firing on all cylinders (if you still drive a gas vehicle, that is). Most people already know the basics of exercise, diet and sleep, and there are plenty of books and other sources for expert advice as it pertains to each unique individual's needs. So, I will share some of the tips that have worked well for me in maintaining my own high-performance model over the years.

See the "Mechanic"

All the money in the world can't buy you back good health.

—Reba McEntire (attributed)

Just because you feel like hammered shit doesn't mean you are hammered shit. When your vehicle sputters and stalls and isn't running as it should, you take it to an auto mechanic, a professional, because it is important for you to have dependable transportation. The same goes for people. When it comes to our bodies and our health, it is our responsibility to be vigilant and proactive.

If you haven't been to the doctor for a while, or you wish to begin a new exercise regimen, get a physical checkup, complete with blood work. It is shocking how many people are low on basic nutrients and vitamins and have no idea. Use the information your doctor provides to make needed changes in your diet, exercise routine or other areas, hopefully before any medications are required. The best way to avoid old Doctor Sawbones is with preventive measures. Understanding what's going on in your body is the key to being able to personalize your preventive measures, thereby making them more effective. With the right information you can fine-tune your diet and exercise routine for your body specifically. This applies to all, regardless of age or experience.

When it comes to your health, having the facts is the all-important first step. My system is to secure paper copies of all my medical lab results and keep them together in a file. When you build a file, you are then able to see how your body is reacting and the patterns that develop over time. You might even find that the lab results are not consistent, which can and does happen. Hell, you might improve or extend your own life a little, simply by watching and paying attention. No one cares about your health as much as you should. Get educated on your own health and build a file on the things that matter to you and your family.

Go for a Spin

Physical fitness is the first requisite of happiness.

—Joseph Pilates

One of the maxims of tai chi is that moving parts don't rust. Keep moving and stay active—that is, commit to some form of exercise routine. You will feel and look better, and you'll be glad you did later in life. If medical conditions are holding you back, they should be dealt with by a professional doctor. Fortunately, laziness and lack of motivation are not medical conditions. (Ahem.) If you are not exercising, it's time to begin. I can almost guarantee that this one adjustment is capable of producing life-changing results.

Stretch. The stretching routine described below is one that I practice first thing each morning.

I mentioned earlier that I often sit on my sports ball while I meditate. My sports ball, or exercise ball, is a large, 36-inch, inflatable rubber ball—big enough to sit or lie on. It is great for practicing balance and building core strength, but also for stretching my neck and back. I may be a little biased, but I believe it is a must-have for everyone.

I lie on my sports ball with my back against the ball and simply let everything fall open—chest up, arms wide, head back. This position reverses the slumped-over posture that so many people develop from sitting at a computer or looking down at their phone for hours on end, day after day. As I move and stretch, I'm able to hear little cracks and pops as areas of my body that are normally closed off begin to open up. For my neck, back, hips, and overall body, rolling out on this ball is a tremendous feeling—almost like floating on air. If you try a sports ball, which I highly recommend, be sure to use it on a soft, padded surface like carpet or a thick mat, especially in the beginning.

Additionally, if you're someone who, like me, gets a pinched nerve in your neck on occasion, then this ball is for you. To stretch my neck, I again lie on the ball with my back down and let my head and shoulders relax backward, keeping my chin tucked. I then smoothly and gently turn my head to the right, then back to center, then to the left, and back to the center. When I do this simple stretch, I always move better and feel better. I was told years ago that surgery was needed on my neck due to old injuries and wear and tear that was causing constant, excruciating pain. Using the sports ball to stretch has eliminated my neck pain completely. I do not fail to do this stretch daily. I can see and feel the benefits and can sure notice the difference when I don't do it.

Walk. If you are just getting started with a fitness routine, keep it simple. Try spending fifteen or twenty minutes a day walking on a treadmill or, better yet, outside in nature, which is a great opportunity to practice the walking meditation technique mentioned earlier. In order to establish a healthy habit, aim for walking at least five days a week. This small change will begin to make a big difference in how you feel. Sitting on your ass couch-locked, or in a chair day after day with no physical activity, is one of the worst things you can do for your health and mood. You are the one who has the power to decide what kind of life you wish to live, so choose wisely. Go for a walk. Feel good. Why not?

Work out. A good workout routine can produce life-changing results when it comes to looking and feeling better. In order to have energy, you must expend energy. In other words, work out. Practice yoga, jump rope, walk, hike, run, swim, spin, push, pull, punch, pedal, lift, climb, crawl—keep moving with whatever you have left. Drag it if you have to and don't ever stop. The problems you will encounter from *not* exercising your body are a much greater burden.

The opposite of slow is fast; of weak is strong; of oppression is empowerment. It is almost impossible not to feel strong and energized as you leave the gym after a good workout. Developing this habit of health and fitness will give you the foundation to then go after whatever you choose. Without good health, everything else quickly becomes secondary. Whatever your size or shape, fitness gains are measured by improvements in *your* body only. Never worry about others—just keep making improvements in your world, little by little taking positive action. Once you establish your routine, keep it moving. You will feel the momentum shift and begin working for you rather than against you. The fun in life is in the action and the interaction, so get to it. There's a saying: People are like sharks; if we stop moving, we die. Let's not let that happen any sooner than necessary. Get the move on—develop a fitness tradition!

My old wrestling buddy Chaz likes to remind me that we have been lifting weights and working out together since high school, which means for over forty years now. It's how we hang out; it's what we do. We lift and train in the gym; not obsessively, but consistently. Working out together over these many years reminds me that great motivation can be realized through having a strong support system, or accountability buddy, to help keep you on track toward your fitness goals.

Accountability buddy or not, decide it is time to make the adjustments needed in your schedule and daily routines; begin and establish fitness as one of your core values. This positive shift will spill over into every other aspect of your life.

Use the Proper Fuel

Those who think they have no time for healthy eating
will sooner or later have to find time for illness.
—Edward Stanley (adapted)

Certainly, if you want to look and feel your best, your diet can and will have a significant impact on your physical and cognitive health. Years of research show that our diet has a significant impact on our overall health and is our best defense against diseases such as diabetes, heart disease and cancer.

Even Alzheimer's and the health of the brain seem to be dramatically influenced by diet. In several nutritional studies conducted in the past decade, researchers have found that people who were genetically prone to cognitive diseases like Alzheimer's could dramatically slow the side effects and even the onset of the disease by improving their diet. The data also revealed that the opposite was true: diets high in saturated fats, of which processed foods, dairy, and fatty meats are primary sources, can exacerbate and speed up the onset of this horrible disease.

Most people are not aware of another surprising fact, which is that up to 90 percent of serotonin, our body's natural antidepressant, is produced in the gut, not the brain. When the bacteria and microbes of the gut are out of balance, it has a negative impact on the production of serotonin, which means we can't be or feel our best. Diet is one of the key factors in shaping the gut microbiome.

There you have it—the type and quality of food we eat is one of our best tools in battling diseases and poor health. Nature has provided for all our vitamin and nutritional needs in the form of fresh food like fruits, nuts, vegetables and meats.

It is almost impossible to eat out at restaurants and eat healthfully. You can try to choose smartly from the menu, but most restaurant food is made with too much fat and too much salt. It might taste good in the moment, but it ends up causing you to consume more calories and sodium than you realize.

In order to eat the right foods, I prefer to cook at home. One of my tricks is to start each week by making a big salad using all fresh, clean, colorful ingredients and storing it in a large plastic resealable bowl. Colorful veggies are loaded with vitamin E and antioxidants that help fight the effects of saturated fats in our body, so the more color, the better. Each day I will make individual salads from that big bowl, adding light dressing, blueberries, egg, avocado, apples, nuts, and other healthy toppings before consuming. This ensures that I get at least one good helping of fresh greens each day. Add a piece of lean beef, salmon or chicken, and you've got a quick and easy meal, packed with the fuel you need to charge ahead at your very best.

A great deal of health and nutrition information is available online that can be customized to your individual diet needs to guide you to a healthier, happier you. Take advantage of it and start developing the right routines. Pay attention to the fuel you put in your body, and make it a priority. Plan and prepare most of your own meals if possible. You will spend less time and money, all while consuming meals packed with the essential nutrients that our bodies need to help us look and feel our very best.

Charge Your Battery

Sleep is the Swiss Army Knife of health. When sleep is deficient, there is sickness and disease. And when sleep is abundant, there is vitality and health.

—Matthew Walker

Our bodies are designed for movement, to go hard and then rest. This is how we grow: we gain and improve our energy by exerting energy. This is also why the quality of our rest or sleep is so important. Sleep is when the body resets and repairs itself. Studies suggest a minimum of seven to eight hours of sleep is required to fully recover from the prior day's activities.

Factors like eating or consuming caffeine too close to bedtime, excessive intake of alcohol, too much screen time right before bed, and of course stress can all negatively impact the amount and quality of our sleep. You don't have to be sleep-deprived for months on end to feel the effects. Being deficient on sleep for just one twenty-four-hour cycle will adversely affect every aspect of your physical wellness.

Remember that everything in life is subject to a rhythm. The sun and moon cycle every twenty-four hours. You too need to regenerate and replenish each night on a rhythmic cycle. If you're having trouble sleeping, create and stick to a set pattern. Develop a calming routine each night at the same time before bed. The meditation and breathing techniques discussed earlier may be helpful for slowing your mind so it can rest.

Then, when the alarm goes off and the morning arrives, realize how the way you spend your first hour sets the tone for the rest of your day. Rather than grabbing your cell phone and plugging in immediately, leverage the peaceful sleep you just had by developing a morning routine that starts your day with a positive and energized vibe. Make your bed, stretch, get in some light exercise, and spend time in prayer or meditation. This is how you start your day off right.

By starting off with an empowering routine, you will realize that you have already accomplished two vitally important energy- and life-giving activities: exercise and prayer. The rest of your day will most certainly reflect this positive and empowering beginning.

Are you ready to see how living with the best version of yourself feels? Exercise, eat clean, and get quality sleep each night. Limit or avoid destructive habits altogether. Let your diet and your lifestyle be your greatest weapons in defending against low energy, poor health and chronic disease. You will look and feel better, be more balanced and productive, and be much happier in the end. As the saying goes, "You're either moving forward or you're backing up." It takes but a small tweak in the way you think to create a new routine that will then ignite the powerful forces of forward momentum. Become empowered; become the driver. Be the one who determines your direction, and carry this wisdom with you. Find out what operating at peak performance can feel like; take the proper steps to care for your vehicle.

The ancient Stoics believed that with each sunset and night we die to the past, if we wake the next day, we are brand new, forgiven of all past sin. With each morning comes a fresh start, a clean slate. What a great way to approach each day. So, focus up—let's make each new day count.

Chapter 6

Sharpen Your Imagination

Every human has four endowments—self-awareness, conscience, independent will, and creative imagination. These give us the ultimate human freedom . . . the power to choose, to respond, to change.

—Stephen Covey

In the spring of 1994, I was living in Arlington, Texas. My house had a small backyard with a six-foot stockade fence separating my yard from the neighbors'. While mowing for the first time that spring, I noticed that a few boards had fallen off the fence and needed to be replaced. So, after I finished weed-eating, I set off to the hardware store to purchase the new lumber. When I finished repairing and replacing the pickets, I was left with an armful of nicely weathered boards in various lengths. I could either toss them in the trash and go back to watching baseball, or I could make something out of them. I chose the latter.

I decided to make some picture frames with my newfound material. I produced four frames of various sizes. Then I remembered that I'd kept our old electric running iron that we used for branding cattle back in the feedlot days—somehow, I knew I would need it again someday. I used the hot iron to make western brands all around the front of the frames. I then inserted mirrors in the frames. I have to admit, I thought they were very cool.

I decided to make a trip to Fort Worth and have a few beers down at the White Elephant Saloon, which is in Cowtown. I took my fancy frames along with me to see if I might find a store interested in buying or carrying them. After a couple of places rejected my work, two sweet ladies in a western craft store took a chance and carried my frames on consignment. I figured if I liked the mirrors, others might also. I was right. Two days later the ladies called and said to come and get my hundred dollars and bring two more mirrors. Apparently, a kind lady had come in and bought two of them with cash.

Since I like making things and working with wood, I immediately saw the potential to earn extra money while having fun. Yes, that's right, I began dismantling my stockade fence one panel at a time.

Around this same time, I married my beautiful (now former) wife. Just before we married, we held a garage sale where we set a few pictures and mirrors around. We made over $800 on the frames alone, never mind all the other junk. This was getting fun.

After a promotion with my company, we were able to move back to Oklahoma, and nine months later our son was born. The missus decided she would set up a booth in a craft mall. We felt this little side business would allow her to stay home with our son, Dalton, rather than take a job in the business world and have to place him in day care. This little hobby turned into a thriving, prosperous side business. We would set up at many different western venues, including PBR (Professional Bull Riders) events, rodeos, AQHA World Quarter Horse Shows, and craft fairs. Our frames—and eventually furniture—were sold to customers from across the U.S. and around the globe, including Canada, New Zealand, Argentina, Brazil and Mexico.

My dad helped us make the frames and furniture, and my wife and I did the detail work, which also involved adding the glass and mirrors. We made some really cool stuff and had quite the system working for several years. Eventually we outgrew the business. My wife wanted to switch careers and move into real estate, which she did very successfully. That and other circumstances caused this business to go by the wayside, but it had carried us through some uncertain times and allowed our family to spend quality time together—not to mention all of the incredible friends and characters we met along the way. All because a few boards fell off my fence in the spring of 1994.

Creativity and imagination are key ingredients for living a richer, fuller life. Many of us know someone who seems to be a creative savant. While this can certainly be the case for the likes of da Vinci and Mozart, for most of us, it's more likely that creativity was sparked by something out of the norm happening—like boards falling off a fence—or simply being excited or curious about something, and then considering the possibilities for that thing.

We can cultivate creativity and imagination by beginning to think in those terms in our day-to-day lives. The more passionate and excited you are about something, the more imaginative you become in your quest toward that passion. If you are excited about something, you are going to think about it a lot, so apply a little focus to your excitement and begin to organize your thoughts. You will start to see creative solutions pop up everywhere.

1. Whatever your topic of curiosity is, brainstorm ideas about it—anything and everything.
2. Document all your ideas, no matter how goofy they may seem.
3. If one of your ideas sparks a little something in you, pursue and investigate that idea.
4. From time to time, revisit your ideas to see what new sparks occur.

The act of writing down your ideas is a catalyst to get the creative juices flowing, and your list will give you a well to draw from when you are feeling idea-dry.

One of my favorite photos of my son is from when he was around four years old. As an only child he was often forced to play alone and entertain himself. I recall the day that

Dalton received a Spider-Man glove that he and his mother had ordered online. He was so excited to get the package open and slide that plastic Spider-Man glove on. This little boy was instantly transformed by a single red rubber glove.

I watched him play for hours with his glove in his imagined world of Spider-Man adventures. But then I noticed my little fella had disappeared, nowhere to be seen. I couldn't find him anywhere. I was about to go in the house to look for him when Dalton reappeared from around the corner. He was wearing the biggest smile, which was visible through the hole in a ski mask he had found. He had also changed into some blue sweatpants, which were tucked into his red knee-high socks and finished off with light blue undies with red piping—worn on the outside, of course. He had pieced together an ensemble that made him look like Spider-Man's much younger, much cuter, miniature sidekick. Okay, I get it, Spider-Man is not real, but at four years old my little boy imagined he was.

Whether it's a red rubber glove or a piece of old wood lying on the ground, begin to see and approach things with possibility and imaginative thinking.

Chapter 7

Set Goals That Pull You

If you are working on something exciting that you really care about, you don't have to be pushed. The vision pulls you.

—Steve Jobs

To paraphrase legendary coach and motivator Lou Holtz: If you're bored with life, you don't have big enough goals.

Goals should be growth- and purpose-driven specifically for you. So often we hear the voice in our head saying "You should do this" or "Don't do that" and end up setting goals based on other people's viewpoints or experience. This is where finding your "why" comes in. We'll discuss finding your why in a moment, but first let us consider this fact. When it comes to building a skyscraper, a home, a car, an airplane, clothes, toys, and thousands upon thousands of other items—from the extremely complex to the very basic—we first must have a design, a set of plans to work from. Constructing the product can then be done in an efficient and organized manner. The same can be said of your life: rather than depending on the whims of circumstance and chance, with the right plan, you can be the one who determines your course.

In 1979, Harvard University researchers surveyed a group of soon-to-graduate students about whether they had developed a plan and established clear goals for their future after graduating from college. The startling results showed that 84 percent had no plan or goals at all, and 13 percent had written goals but had no steps to take to attain them. Only 3 percent had clearly documented goals with steps to take toward each. These were detailed plans documented with pen and paper, showing exactly what they wanted and how they would go about getting it. They created a map or playbook to build the future they desired. The remarkable thing was that ten years later, when researchers observed the same individuals, they found that the 3 percent who had detailed goals and a clear plan to attain them earned on average *ten times more than the rest.* Knowing this, which group would you prefer to be in?

The vast majority of great authors and motivational speakers, not to mention the plethora of books on the subjects of success, personal growth, and happiness, tell you to begin by finding and setting the right goals, and then documenting and executing on the steps required to reach them. Henry Ford once said that no goal is too big if you break it down into enough parts. It makes perfect sense. This idea of goal setting is not a new concept and carries immense power. It would be wise and provide a significant advantage for you to not only use it, but to become an expert at it. No matter what stage of life you are in, you can and should be the one who decides what your path forward will look like. We accomplish this by having a well-documented strategy or plan toward our worthwhile goals. Ask yourself if it is important enough for you to take a few minutes and create a plan that you can continue to sharpen and hone as you work toward your purpose. This is how you go after something and create powerful forces toward its attainment.

Brainstorm possible goals. The first thing we must do is to identify and define more clearly than ever before what it is we really want and, perhaps more importantly, why we want it.

Ask yourself two critical questions:

- What positive and empowering thing will I do next? And...
- Why?

Then, brainstorm and document possible answers to these two questions. What goal would get your juices flowing and excite you to the point that you would enjoy thinking about and working toward its attainment? What would be your dream job, dream house or dream business? What motivates you, where do you want to go, what would you like to have and what do you want to be? Dream big or not—it's all for you to decide. Take the time to think about what is important to you, then write it all down and meditate on these answers.

Try to be creative when coming up with possible goals. Have fun with the process. Get those imaginative juices flowing. Start to design and establish a foundation for the type of life you want through the goals you set for yourself.

Choose master goals. Once you have a list of possible goals, find out what your *master* goals are. A master goal is something that gets you charged up about going after it. This is the goal you are excited about spending your time and efforts toward. It might even keep you up at night thinking about it.

Some people will know exactly what it is I'm talking about and know exactly what they are after, in much the same way I knew writing this book was my next master goal. If this sounds like your case, perfect; document that goal, apply these methods, then hammer down. Don't look back, and never give up.

Others will struggle in the beginning of this process. If you find you are having difficulty discovering your master goal, it may be helpful to reflect on your past. What things have you been skilled at and shown an interest in? Think about the things that have inspired and energized you, made you excited or brought you joy.

Still, others may wish to search for new and exciting experiences never yet attempted or even dreamed of. Go for it. Document your desire and begin your journey; it is never too late to get started.

Being inspired about something, like I was about completing this book, creates a force that cannot and will not be denied. A quote by Benjamin Disraeli sums it up perfectly: "Nothing can resist a will that will stake even [its own] existence on its fulfillment." Set goals worth working for, that inspire you, that make you excited when you think about working on them. When you are inspired by your goals you will be more likely to spend the time necessary for their attainment. This is the reason your "why" is so important.

As someone once said, "If your why don't make you cry, then it's not your why."

Some people prefer to have many goals and categorize them into personal, material and financial compartments. While I document these goals in my notebook, I prefer to drill down and laser focus on one *master* goal at a time. Obviously, my most recent master goal and sole purpose was to complete the manuscript for *Hammer Down* and see it turned into a book. My ultimate objective in writing this book was the sincere hope that it will inspire and show others how to work toward their own goals and dreams. Anyone can discover what it feels like to be excited in their pursuit of something they deem important. Let's face it, we can't achieve "it" if we don't define clearly what "it" is.

Many cry for "wants" and "haves," but very few cry for "do's" and become. Be one of the few. Set goals based on desired experiences and relationships as well as things you want to do or wish to be. This is how you gain direction and become the driver of your future.

Focus on positive goals. In setting goals, it may first be helpful to make a list of things you want to stop doing or being. Look back over the past months or even years and determine which activities or habits are not propelling you forward or, worse, are holding you back. You may wish to have a goal that involves eliminating a bad habit, such as stopping smoking or drinking, losing weight, or getting out of debt. That's terrific. However, if you are truly committed to making the change occur, you will want to replace the old routine with a new, positive routine.

We should all know by now that we attract what we think about. The thing we fear the most and try to avoid is the exact thing we attract into our lives. By implementing a new positive habit to replace an old one—such as beginning an exercise routine, learning to cook, taking yoga, meditating, painting, or even skydiving—your chances of success improve substantially.

For example, say you have a master goal of paying off debt. Instead of focusing on the debt, shift your thought to the positive desired state—financial freedom and all it implies. This positive master goal could lead you to identify a second source of income through creative new ways of thinking. At this point don't worry about the "how"; just know that if you have found your "why," the "how" will be revealed through your persistence. Keeping your focus on the positive will help you gain momentum toward your objective.

Document your goals. As mentioned, I prefer to have one master goal at a time. Of course, I document the many other ideas that may one day become master goals, but I set them aside until I can spend the time and energy necessary to give them the attention they deserve. I consider my master goal a living document, always updating and sharpening the steps. As I discover new possibilities that can help me get closer to my goal, I write them down. Occasionally, you may want to make your master goals larger or more ambitious, tweaking them as you acquire additional information and feedback in the quest toward your purpose.

I find it is also a good idea to have a separate to-do list for everyday chores—such as cleaning out the garage and changing the oil in the car. Maintaining separate lists will help keep your master goal isolated and targeted toward your growth, excitement and contribution, not mixed in with a list of chores that need to be completed. I am also a big believer in capturing ideas from my brainstorming or other creative thoughts and solutions in my notebook. My son keeps his own lists on his phone; I still prefer pen and a yellow legal pad. Famed billionaire investor, entrepreneur and inventor Richard Branson considers the notebook where he logs his thoughts and ideas to be one of his most prized possessions.

Define Your Power Steps

If it's important, you will find a way.
If it's not, you will find an excuse.
—Ryan Blair

Once you find your objective—your master goal—and your reason why, it's time to dissect your goals into power steps. I recommend you come up with as many power steps as possible in reaching your goal—at least twenty. That may sound like a lot, but by forcing your mind to come up with this many, no matter how silly some may sound, it will help you start to think outside the box when looking for innovative opportunities.

Without direction, without a plan, the chances of success are minimal. Try going to the grocery store without a list of items to buy. Your chances of getting home with everything you need are slim; there are too many distractions and choices to remember what was important earlier. Life is much the same. Having a plan, a shopping list, ensures success. Not having a plan means indecision and uncertainty, which creates fear and inefficiency. After carefully considering your course and having a plan, you can choose to be decisive and deliberate in your actions. You just need a simple list of things that are important to you and a path for their attainment.

To measure progress toward your master goal, establish a clear starting point and a concrete date for attainment. *This is where I am today. This is where I want to be a year from now.* And of course, don't forget the power steps: *This is what I'm willing to do to get there.* You need to be honest and realistic in both your assessment of where you are now and where you want to end up. It's great to dream big and have huge goals; you definitely should. You also need to be realistic about the work involved. Are you willing to do all that is required to achieve that big goal? If your why is truly your why, the answer will be *hell, yes!*

You create momentum by reviewing and working on the small, clearly defined steps you will take each day to reach your goal. We call these "power steps" because the power lies in the implementation of each step. With the completion of each power step, you begin to gather momentum toward your goal. Once again, we are applying the principles of leverage—small changes that can produce huge results.

As you measure progress, you may be tempted to compare yourself to others. Don't. Compare yourself only to your own goals, progress and standards. Did you do better today than yesterday? Did you execute against your plan?

When I first set writing this book as my master goal, I did not truly comprehend the number of hours that would be required in researching, writing and revising over and over, not to mention the hours spent staring at the computer screen. But, like most things worthwhile, I figured it required commitment and determination, and I knew I had plenty of that. So, I wrote the words "Write a book," as well as the power steps I needed to do so. It was set; I was to become an author in 2019.

I began to work on this goal that very moment and have not looked back since. It is always with me, whether I am working on it or not. It is right there as I wait to see or hear something inspiring that might further my quest to add value for the reader. Without documenting my goal to write this book and formulating a plan for its completion, I would never have made it this far. The momentum I've created by documenting and working on my goal daily has carried me much further and more quickly than I would have ever believed possible. Many times, the words come to me at 3 a.m. No matter; I embrace the energy and delve into the work with enthusiasm. Other times, the words just don't come, and progress is slow. It has been a remarkable journey and a truly uplifting experience. Regardless of any perceived measure of commercial or ego-driven success, it has been worth every second.

Visualize Attaining Your Goals

First say to yourself what you would be;

and then do what you have to do.

—Epictetus

As soon as you have established your master goal(s) and the steps you need to take, document each goal clearly with a firm date for attainment, and then sign and date the document. At this point, begin to visualize in your mind what the attainment of your desired goal will look and feel like. Continue to imagine what it will be like to have your goal accomplished. Feel the energy of that thought daily.

I myself continue to imagine what finishing my first book will feel like: the sense of accomplishment that I will have knowing my work will inspire someone to make positive changes, the feeling of holding in my hands a book that I created, knowing it will be a family treasure for my son and future grandkids.

This imagined feeling of already having achieved your goal is powerful. It provides the fuel to keep you going when the ego begins to allow doubt and unwanted thoughts to distract you from your purpose. This is an empowering way to go through your day. Develop your goals around the type of lifestyle you wish to have and the person you wish to be. Then get to work; believe you will have this lifestyle and believe that in your very core. This is the tremendous benefit of having the right goal: you always have something inspiring to direct your efforts toward. Once you find this, whatever anyone may say, keep pushing forward toward your objective, power step by power step.

Be Determined, But Flexible

The measure of intelligence is the ability to change.

—Anonymous

It is imperative to have a goal, a target, a plan—or else the ego takes over and the brain gets lost in its own created chaos. You need the persistence and endurance to pursue that goal, but you also need the ability to adapt to the ever-changing situations of daily life. In the infamous words of Iron Mike Tyson, "Everyone has a plan until they get punched in the mouth." The ability to adapt as you receive new information is a valuable skill to develop. Whether it's getting hit in the mouth or discovering something isn't working, realize and appreciate that it's all feedback.

Having an open mind, valuing new information and adapting accordingly creates an open state of fluidity that allows for improved recognition of opportunities. Stay on course toward your goals, but be flexible in response to the ever-changing and unpredictable circumstances that occur in life. When it comes to things you cannot change, develop a "roll with it" attitude. Save your energy for what you can impact and accept the rest as it is. That doesn't mean give up at the first sign of resistance—quite the contrary. Hitting resistance is when you likely want to either dig in and *hammer down* or reassess the situation and adjust your approach if necessary. Let me give you an example.

I was interviewing for my first job in the corporate world, a sales position for the Oscar Mayer company, then part of General Foods. The position came with a nice salary, company car, insurance, retirement package—the works. I had the first interview, then I went back for a second interview, then a third. I knew I had a good shot, and this position was the exact thing I needed at the exact right time. After the farm crisis in the early 1980s, we came very close to losing the ranch, and I was in need of work. A chance at a career with a strong national company was just what the doctor ordered.

The only problem was, I didn't get the position. I received a call one afternoon telling me that after much consideration, they'd decided to go with the other candidate, who was a current General Foods employee. I admit, I was devastated for about fifteen minutes. Then the devastation turned into anger, which I channeled into action.

Thirty minutes after getting the call telling me I didn't get the position, I called Oscar Mayer's headquarters in Madison, Wisconsin, and asked for the head of the human resources department. I explained to the nice lady that after an extensive interview process, I'd come in second place. I wondered if she might review my file and consider me for a position with the company elsewhere in the U.S. I really wanted the job, and I was ready to go anywhere. The HR director said she appreciated my call and my professional approach, then asked that I call the regional office where I had interviewed and ask them to forward my information to the company's home office.

So, one hour after I had been told no on the position, I was calling back the manager who had declined my hire. The instant the secretary answered the phone and recognized my voice, she began to panic, thinking I was bitter about the decision. I interrupted her as quickly as I could and assured her my intentions were purely professional; I then explained the situation. After hearing my story and relaying it to the manager, she returned and indicated they would be happy to forward my information.

The next day, unexpectedly, I received another call, this time telling me they had decided to offer me the position I had interviewed for and wanted all along. The manager had *reversed his decision* because of my tenacity. I will never forget the feeling I had after this phone call: I literally jumped with joy and then collapsed with tears of relief. I had poured all my energy and focus into this process for weeks. After being told no the day before, somehow the position was now mine. I was in total disbelief; it felt like divine intervention. Those thirty minutes of being tenacious changed the trajectory of my life forever.

Sometimes rejection and the word "no" simply mean more information is required. Don't give up too easily on things you consider worthwhile. In this case I was able to find a way around the rejection, a way to keep the process alive for me, by refusing to give up and by looking for creative alternatives. The resulting energy worked for me in a remarkable, if not miraculous, fashion. This position launched a successful fifteen-year career.

Persistence and flexibility go hand in hand. Know your ultimate goal, but be open to different ways of achieving it.

As I learned while attending a Franklin Planner seminar in the mid-1990s, documenting your goals and having a plan for their success creates something magical within you that propels you toward what you desire. I cannot stress enough how this practice can impact every aspect of your life for the better. Did I reach all the goals I had set for myself back then? No, but it is remarkable how close I came to the exact things I documented. When you combine a little persistence and flexibility with this process, you will begin to see the benefits quickly. So stop now. Go through this process yourself and, after some serious consideration, drill down to one or two master goals that you would be excited, even passionate, about working toward. Constantly imagine and envision what having your goal will be like. Try to invoke this feeling in your very core on a daily basis, and as you begin to discover new and imaginative ways to reach your purpose, write them down!

Chapter 8

Hammer Down

The way to get started is to quit talking and begin doing.

—Walt Disney

During my first year as an insurance agent, I was fortunate enough to win the all-star award for my sales performance, a recognition that included an incredible trip to Australia. In this organization it was rare to see a brand-new agent have this kind of success, so one of the managers from another region asked me to speak at a sales meeting about how I was generating so much activity. I reluctantly accepted his invitation, although at the time I had no idea what I would say. The majority of my audience would be sales professionals with many years of experience. What did I have to offer them?

On my drive back to the office I tried to think of what I might say, and then suddenly began to tremble at the thought of the whole thing. That evening, I started analyzing what I was doing that allowed me to create and close so much business. I remembered a question that I had been asked a week earlier while I was in the office of a local bank president. He was curious to know how I was achieving this level of success in my new career. One of his former employees had tried to be an agent around the same time I was hired.

Walking in I had noticed some files and a stack of mail on his desk. My answer to him was this: "Please take no offense, but this stack of papers on your desk? By this time of the day, I would have been through all that mail, thrown away all the unnecessary crap, filed what needed to be filed, and delegated or acted on what needed action. I don't mill around the task; I get into it with a laser focus. My desk stays clear for the next deal."

After leaving that appointment, I realized that I was working fewer hours than my counterparts (I would leave the office at noon practically every day), but at this point I was outproducing them all. I realized that I didn't get distracted with all the pointless emails, requests, and reams of unnecessary information and paperwork that came with the business. Managers, underwriters, and even some clients will have you covered up in reports, requests, and what-if scenarios that produce little to no value. I like to refer to this condition as being "tangled up in your underwear." I was hired as an independent contractor, and I preferred to do it my way, which was to make sure I understood the client's needs and ethically acted in their best interest, period. This I learned from my dad as well as from my many years in sales with Kraft Foods.

I learned to hit the high spots and keep moving. In my mind, everyone needed our product—insurance—and I wanted to be out in the world prospecting, be it at my kid's little league games, at the gym in the evenings, or at a cow auction on Saturday. I was getting paid to sell, and that's what I did. I tried to ask the right questions and convey the right things to earn people's confidence in my integrity and my knowledge of the business. I believed then as I do now that the honesty and strong ethics I learned as a youth have always been my greatest assets—those and the no-fear, no-quit attitude I have when I set my mind to something I believe in.

Perhaps one of my other fortes was my ability to comprehend complicated information, no matter how long it might take, and then get it down to the point where I could communicate it in simple terms. My goal was to present the information in a fashion that made it easy for the customer to understand so they could make an informed decision, not to confuse them with endless options and irrelevant details. If I'd done my job of listening to the customer to begin with, I already had a good idea of which products they needed.

Most of my selling was done not across the desk but in casual conversations out and about in the world. I recall many times taking my pickup, horse and trailer and helping my customers gather cattle off wheat or grass pastures. I did this expecting nothing in return besides friendship and fellowship. When they eventually needed some type of insurance product or had a question, I knew who they would call. The office was just the place they came to sign paperwork. I found this approach to be very effective, perhaps because that is what I would like to see if I were in the customer's shoes—someone who shows up, talks plain and keeps it simple.

As I began working on my presentation, in addition to noticing the things I did, I also began to notice the things I *didn't* do. They seemed equally important. I did not stand around for an hour drinking coffee, reading the paper, or chatting with the assistants about the latest office gossip. I was always in the office early, and I would immediately shift into a mode of intensely focused effort. My assistant always dove right into this mode as well. We were a team. "I caught 'em and she cleaned 'em" was a fishing metaphor I liked to use. (Dee, if you're reading this, you are and were the best. We made a great team. Thank you once again.)

The day came for me to give my presentation. I was feeling pretty good because I felt I had something to share that would be of value to those who would apply my simple philosophy: hammer down.

The Hammer Down Method

A river cuts through rock, not because of its power,

but because of its persistence.

—James N. Watkins

Each day we are all given the precious gift of twenty-four hours, or 1,440 minutes. The time can't be saved or stored; it must be spent or it's gone forever, never to be regained. Up to half of this time is spent sleeping, feeding and cleaning ourselves. Which leaves us with just over 700 minutes each day to accomplish something productive. When you stop to consider how many of those minutes are spent sitting in traffic, on your phone, at your computer, or watching TV, obviously, how you spend the remaining few minutes of your day is of critical importance when it comes to the level of success you will experience at anything. Over the years I have found that by applying small intervals of focused, concentrated effort on a task, I become highly effective at conquering my objective, little by little. You probably have heard the saying "All things in moderation." As it turns out, that goes for moderation as well! I have been using the following radical action technique for much of my life.

In essence, once you've found your master goal (or other clearly defined objective), develop a daily routine that commits a minimum of fifteen minutes of focused action on the power steps that lead to that goal. All energy is channeled into one sharp point toward your purpose. This is called concentration. Practice it, learn it and integrate it into everything you do. We are not talking about fifteen minutes of halfhearted effort. It should be laser-focused, all-in and without distraction. By breaking down your large goal into small actionable steps, you can develop momentum as you complete each step. Some days you may end up working hours on your particular goal, but fifteen minutes of concentrated action toward each step is all I actually commit. I find that by compartmentalizing the large tasks into small intervals, the objective becomes more manageable as I begin to develop a rhythm of chipping away at whatever I'm working on.

Think about what you might accomplish in a year if you commit just fifteen minutes a day of radical action: you can literally read the Bible cover to cover, learn a new language or even write a book. I taught myself how to play the guitar this way. Make the choice to wake up every morning and do as many pushups as you can in fifteen minutes; after one year, let's just say you will look and feel a lot different.

My routine as an insurance agent was to get to the office before anyone else, which always gave me a feeling of being ahead of the pack. I would return calls and respond to any unanswered messages from the day before. The key was to sharpen my message and to ask the right questions in order to uncover and resolve the needs of my clients.

This is how I was able to leverage additional sales across our different lines of business.

Learn to concentrate your energies on a specific goal in order to engage the forces of momentum. What do I mean by momentum? Merriam-Webster defines it as "the strength or force that allows something to continue or grow stronger and faster as time passes." It's the basic law of physics: mass in motion. Like that bicycle lying in the yard, we don't amount to much until we get moving toward something, then the momentum kicks in and it gets easier. We may have to work a little harder in the beginning, but then we are carried forward in an almost effortless fashion. Once you reach this balance, stay with it and keep moving toward your purpose.

Throughout these pages we have discussed the importance of getting and keeping momentum working for us. This is key if we want to reach our master goals. We can change and redirect momentum by making small positive adjustments in our daily routines and habits and by repeating that day after day until the positive energy flows freely in our direction. Find what works, then repeat it over and over. This is how we can use momentum to build a legacy. A commitment of fifteen minutes of targeted action daily is all it takes to get started.

Since we now have the tools we need to gain control over our direction, let's choose to move and create momentum in a forward fashion. In order for positive momentum to occur, two other ingredients are necessary: efficiency and enthusiasm. When you combine these with positive motion, you create forward momentum. The more efficient and enthusiastic you are in your action, the more positive momentum you create.

Pursue Efficiency

Efficiency is a great secret that can drop us right into our ideal life path, but it is a hard one to practice and something that takes constant maintenance and work.

—Tara Stiles

When you begin to think in terms of efficiency and momentum, positive changes begin to occur. This can be a powerful shift.

Avoid distractions. If you wish to be more efficient and productive in reaching your goals, you must learn to eliminate and avoid distractions. This is a major barrier for many people due to the plethora of text messages, emails, social media, and marketing information that is directed at us on a constant basis. And that's before you ever turn on the TV to catch the news or your favorite sitcom.

Our objective should be to use information and technology as a benefit instead of letting it drag us and our goals into a torrent of continuous distractions. Hit the delete button on time-killing, stress-creating clutter and replace it with goal-getting activities. How important are your goals to you? Is it worth sacrificing a continuous stream of commercials and mindless crap served up as entertainment? Remember, we get only 1,440 minutes each day. Become efficient; you only have to eliminate the distractions and put your effort toward the right things.

Eliminate the unnecessary. When considering ways to improve your efficiency, it helps to think in terms of activities that are wasting effort, money and time. Look for activities that can be eliminated completely, and take the necessary steps to begin removing these from your daily life. For the activities that cannot be eliminated altogether, look for ways to improve on them, limit them, or replace them with momentum-creating action (remember your power steps) that move you closer to your goals.

There are many articles, videos and books out there that discuss ways to become more efficient in your life. One of my favorites is the *New York Times* bestselling book *The 4-Hour Workweek* by Timothy Ferriss. Tim offers a tremendous amount of advice, as well as tricks and methods that you can implement immediately to become more efficient and effective in your everyday life—from meal prep to configuring your smartphone. His books and podcast have been motivating and most helpful in improving efficiency in my life.

Find leverage points. We can all discover adjustments we can make to improve our use of the time that we have each day. One way is to look for leverage points—places you can do more with less. For example, as mentioned in the previous paragraph, I enjoy listening to Tim Ferriss's podcast, in which he interviews elite performers in various fields of expertise. Doing this while in my car driving, or even at the gym while working out, is a great way to leverage time in order to learn about topics that are of interest to me. Learning to value and manage your time is key to reducing stress and being effective at leveraging your efforts.

Look for scale efficiencies. Imagine this scenario for a moment: you enter a bit of information into your computer and—"Presto!"—your new 3D printer goes to work constructing a beautiful trinket. You decide to put it on a string and wear it around your neck. People begin to ask you about it and comment they would like to have one. The lightbulb comes on, and you ask yourself, *How can I make a bunch of these little things?* They are worth only about $5, but if you could find a way to duplicate the original as effectively and efficiently as possible, maybe, just maybe, this could become a business.

This is how fortunes are built: by developing creative ideas on a small scale and then applying that formula on a larger scale—that is, by finding efficiencies. The secret is to realize the opportunities are there if you can remove distractions and self-imposed limitations long enough to notice them.

Communicate clearly and honestly. One other ingredient useful in becoming more efficient is good communication skills. This skill too can be developed with practice and minor adjustments in the way you think. Learn to be clear in your communications; follow up and confirm details so that wasted time and effort are kept to a minimum. Be the person who is known for being honest at all costs, who keeps your word and who is dependable. It will pay huge dividends throughout your lifetime.

Cultivate Enthusiasm

Enthusiasm is the yeast that makes your hopes shine to the stars. Enthusiasm is the sparkle in your eyes, the swing in your gait. The grip of your hand, the irresistible surge of will and energy to execute your ideas.

—Henry Ford (attributed)

At this point you should be feeling excited and enthusiastic about embracing a renewed focus toward your desires. That's right. The other ingredient necessary to create the kind of momentum we want is enthusiasm. To have enthusiasm, your state of mind must be positive. Being inspired and excited about something creates enthusiasm. In my opinion, there is no better feeling in the world. This is the benefit and power that comes with working toward the right goal: the more action and effort you apply toward it, the more your enthusiasm builds.

With the right attitude and the right techniques, you have the formula for success. Unleash these powerful forces in your world. All success is a result of focused, unwavering desire mixed with determined, enthusiastic action. When you apply this knowledge and these methods together toward your clearly defined goals, you forge a wave of energy that cannot be denied.

In the previous chapters we discussed techniques that, when applied and combined, will at the very minimum help you live a more productive and fulfilling life. However, the upside that can be realized by applying these wisdoms is limited only by your desire and imagination. When you combine and apply these recommendations, you will begin to feel the improved momentum and energy quickly. It will give you a road map to hammer down like never before. You'll begin to feel like you are on a mission and nothing can stop you. You only need a worthy target, a master goal to begin the application of these powerful principles.

The choice is yours. You can wake tomorrow and remain in your same old routines, wandering around from chore to chore, or you can wake up with a fresh new perspective—a different, better way to live and approach each and every day.

ђ

Chapter 9

Create Your Circle

With harmony, small things grow;

without harmony, great things decay.

—Sallust (adapted)

In the heat of the summer the year I turned seventeen, we had a truckload of cattle coming in from New Mexico. Our buyer had mentioned these cattle were a little wild but that he had bought them at a bargain. *Oh boy,* I thought. I had seen some of his bargains before.

As we began to unload the nervous critters, I could see he was right—they were jumpy as all get out. They were slamming against gates, bucking, kicking and slinging cow shit everywhere as they charged off that truck. I noticed right away what the problem was: 90 percent of them were Brahmas, the same kind they use in the PBR events as bucking bulls—the ones with big humps, long ears and horns. These cattle looked more like giant jackrabbits than cows. A couple had already effortlessly jumped the fence into the horse lot. I determined that this herd must not have been around people much since they came from such big rough country. It takes a lot of acreage to run cattle in New Mexico due to the rough, dry climate and lack of vegetation.

As soon as all the cattle were counted and off the truck, my job was to gather them back around into the sorting pen and check for any sick or injured animals that needed to be doctored. This task was usually done on foot; however, this day I was thinking maybe I'd better saddle my horse. But I decided to open the gate and see if I could manage without all that hassle. As I entered the dusty lot, I immediately noticed this big red tiger-striped Brahma bull walking straight toward me. He looked like the devil himself. For a split second I thought, *Run for the fence, man!* But then I saw something: as wild and crazy looking as this big creature was, he was acting strangely curious.

I stood perfectly still with my hand out for him to sniff. He was just a couple feet away and inching closer, albeit skittishly. I knew he could murder me right then and there if he decided to, but I could also see his curiosity in me, and for all I knew, he could see my interest in him. The other cattle were locked in a trance watching me and this red bull interact, as if waiting for his signal to erupt into a massive explosion of nervous energy. Thankfully, and to my surprise, he gave no such signal.

He began to sniff the back of my hand, and I started rubbing his nose a little. *This is the same way I'd work with a young horse,* I thought.

It took quite a while, but I had that big red bull as calm and relaxed as he could be. I could pet and rub him all over; he was like a big teddy bear. He looked like the meanest, craziest animal I had ever seen, but here I was, pushing and petting on him like an old dog. I would scratch his neck a little and he would hang his big ole head and close his eyes and enjoy every second of it. The moment I would stop he would open his eyes as if to say, "Well, why'd you stop?" Then I'd scratch him again and he would shut his eyes again. This went on until we were pals.

I could hardly believe what was happening. At that moment I noticed another amazing thing. It was like all those other cattle that had been watching and waiting to explode let out a collective exhale of relief. (Them and me both.) I noticed how they seemed to change and relax all at once into a different pen of cattle—all because they saw that big red bull acting calm and relaxed. They watched my every move as I used a piece of old nylon hay twine around the bull's neck to urge him through the gate, which he did by following me, twine not useful or needed. That bull followed me into the sorting alley, and the rest of the herd slipped right in behind him. I never would have believed it. I led the whole bunch into that pen smooth as butter. That was the first and last time that ever happened. I thought about how that bull calmed all those other cattle down so quickly by his own relaxed manner. Considering how wild and crazy those cattle were coming off that truck, I thought, *Damn, now that was cool.*

Think about what emotions you are projecting, and the impact they have on others and yourself. Is it a relaxed and confident energy, or is it wild and nervous? Do you easily gravitate into anger and the "poor pitiful me" cycle? Are you ready to feel the quiet calm of confidence and empowerment?

As you begin to develop more awareness and balance in your life, you will start to notice activities, and even people, that are no longer in line with your values and objectives. You must decide which relationships are positive and empowering, which ones drain precious energy, and which might even risk the whole mission toward your desires. The old saying "misery loves company" really is true.

Are you hanging out with people who encourage and support your goals, the life-givers? Or are you hanging out with negative, even dangerous, people who want to rob you of your precious life energy? The people we surround ourselves with will significantly impact how happy we are as well as the level of success we are able to experience, period.

If what I'm saying sounds familiar, it is being repeated here to emphasize once again the significant impact that being around the right people can have. This one thing can provide a shortcut on your path to success, sort of like when I displayed patience and took the time to connect with the right animal in that pen of cattle and then the momentum shifted and flooded in my direction.

Let's face it: at times our friends, family and significant others can be irritating and negative. Instead of trying to change them, adjust your reaction to them in order to project what you ultimately want, which are things like harmony, respect, inspiration and even patience. Encourage and support others in their dreams and ask them to do the same for you. Surrounding yourself with people who support and believe in your goals is a huge advantage.

If you want to go to the next level, find people who have similar dreams and desires and are going after the same goals you are. Let's say your dream is to be a musician. It may help to hang out with other folks wishing to become musicians and share some tricks of the trade while you are on your journey.

If you want to go to the next level still, find a mentor to help you—someone who has already done what you are dreaming of, someone who has already been successful at what you are trying to achieve. This is the ultimate advantage—someone who's "been there and done that" to help you navigate the path.

These are the relationships that will propel you toward your goals much faster.

I am not saying that you will not reach your goals without surrounding yourself with like-minded people. You may very well be a loner and want to do it all on your own.

Frankly, being able to count on yourself to hammer down when you need to is a great quality to have. But also consider that having a genuine curiosity in your area of interest and sharing it with someone who has that same curiosity, seemingly creates the energy of a third person. Use this knowledge and form of leverage to your advantage. It too carries big power.

Thinking back on that gentle red bull reminds me of two lessons—first, that most things are not as they appear to be. We really can't judge a book by its cover because we all have inherent biases blocking our view. We must look and dig deeper. And second, the energy we project is reflected back by those around us. Get and keep the positive feedback loop going by projecting good thoughts and energy, and then find and associate with others who wish to do the same.

ħ

Chapter 10

Endure Onward

Rejoice always, pray continually, and

give thanks in all circumstances.

—1 Thessalonians 5:16–18

During my career as an insurance agent, we had many tornadoes in Oklahoma—there's a reason they call it Tornado Alley. The worst storm took place on May 24, 2011, now on record as the largest and deadliest tornado outbreak in history; eleven people, including small children, lost their lives that day. With five monster tornadoes and winds of up to 280 miles per hour, hundreds of people were severely injured; in fact, it was not clear how so many survived the massive devastation that was unleashed on our communities.

After the storm passed, I immediately drove out to check on and help my clients. Everyone, everywhere, seemed to be in a state of shock and bewilderment. The scene before us all was one of immense destruction. I remember thinking the devastation must be similar to that of an air raid bombing, like our soldiers saw in Vietnam and early during the Iraq War.

It was like a scene from a movie as first responders and the National Guard rolled up to secure the damaged areas so the search for survivors and recovery of victims could begin. Miraculously, none of my family, friends, or clients lost their lives. I did, however, have many clients who lost everything else. Houses, belongings, cars, and even family pets were swept away.

My first stop was to see my lifelong friends and clients Charles and Vicki, who lost everything that day. When the tornado descended upon their farm, Vicki was under the stairs in the home. The tornado lifted the house off the foundation; then, when it and several outbuildings exploded into a million pieces of flying debris, Vicki was blown out into the yard. It is hard to imagine how, but, by the hand of God, she survived the ordeal without critical injury, though she was badly shaken, bruised and in a state of severe shock.

I had many more client stops ahead of me. The volume of customers suffering losses was staggering. We had to prioritize the worst cases first and get to the rest as soon as the debris and dust settled. I proceeded to total loss after total loss. Families were waiting for me and our team of adjusters to explain their coverage and provide immediate funds for basic living expenses; many had nothing left but the clothes on their back.

This day is burned into my mind forever due to the unbelievable magnitude of destruction, and perhaps more so due to the volume and intensity of human emotion we were exposed to in such a short period. I don't have a degree in psychology but felt like I earned the armchair version after dealing with the aftermath from that catastrophic event—not only from helping our customers but also from handling and sorting through the mountain of bureaucracy from headquarters. This storm put smaller insurance companies out of business, and it took a toll on our organization as well.

Looking back on that period, it was baptism by fire, or in this case by EF5 tornadoes. It felt good knowing we were going to be able to help these survivors rebuild and get back on their feet, but I also understood that it was impossible to replace everything. And, as we all do, many times customers had chosen the less expensive coverage in order to save money, often against my advice. A lower premium is great until an unforeseen tragedy happens and you realize some things are not adequately covered. This situation becomes tenuous and difficult for the client and the agent, since most folks, understandably, are reluctant to blame themselves come claim time.

The point is, unexpected, completely crazy and horrible shit is going to occur throughout your lifetime. How we choose to respond after surviving the storm is just that—a choice.

Later that day I eased into the remains of another neighborhood (or what used to be a neighborhood) where I had a family of four with a total loss—house, cars, clothes—everything gone. I remember walking up the driveway and meeting them where their house once stood. While everyone appeared unharmed, all were in tears and a state of shock over the loss. I tried to assure them that their coverage was adequate and that everything was covered to rebuild back to new. I had hoped this would help calm them a little, but it did not seem to matter. They had barely escaped with their lives and were understandably traumatized by this overwhelming loss. After delivering the family a payment for basic necessities, I have to admit I left in tears as well.

On to my last stop of the day, my buddy Chris's house (or at least where he used to have a house). His family too was in the yard, but the scene was completely different from what I had experienced just a few minutes earlier. While the family seemed in shock, everyone was smiling—they were so thankful to be alive, it was like they hardly noticed their beautiful home was gone. When I stepped out of my truck, I was met with a hug and a smile from my big Indian friend. I returned the hug with enthusiasm since they all came so close to losing their lives. I also needed and appreciated the lift in spirits.

I'll never forget what Chris said next. He looked at his beautiful wife, Carrie, and with his big ole smile said,

"Well, honey, I guess we're getting all new shit." What an attitude! I wondered if I would be able to handle this situation the same way. The kids were playing and messing around, even laughing, in the now debris-scattered yard. It was a shocking contrast to my previous stop. Chris's five family members rode out the tornado in a storm shelter in the garage. This in-ground shelter was literally all that survived of their possessions. It had saved the entire family, but they didn't even have an extra pair of underwear. Everything was gone, and yet the way they just rolled with their situation—I will never forget the courage and kindness that was displayed by my friend and his family in their time of crisis.

There are many stories of heroism and survival from that day, from the first responders to friends and neighbors and even people coming into Oklahoma from other states to help prevent more loss and clean up after the horrific event. The communities affected have since been rebuilt and continue to thrive. When Chris and his family moved from the area, he dug up the storm shelter that saved his loved ones and took it with him to his current home. I think we can all appreciate and understand his attachment.

I continue to reflect on how he and so many others handled this type of sudden loss and utter devastation. It is truly an amazing thing when you see the human spirit exposed to such massive tragedy and, after surviving it, shine stronger and brighter than ever. The incredible energy and life that surrounded my friend and his family that afternoon had an instant effect on me. As I drove off, I thought, *Man, did I ever need that.*

Life has a way of knocking the air out of you. If you're still alive, get up, get going and begin again. Do the best you can with what you have, then tomorrow, do that again. The ability to accept what is and then build and roll on from there is a precious skill to acquire and develop.

At one point or another we will all feel victimized. The best advice is to resist this temptation. Allowing yourself to succumb to the title "victim" and having others feel sorry for you may make you feel all warm inside, but it is a sure way to spiral into self-pity, negativity, and low energy—basically the exact opposite direction that you and I want to be heading, which is upward and onward.

Many people love to feel sorry for themselves, to play the victim, to blame someone else for their unhappiness. Some even like to blame God. Our society encourages this behavior. We seek out victims or groups of supposed victims in order to encourage ourselves and others to feel like victims. Don't get me wrong. People who have suffered from war, violence, assaults, accidents, illness and, yes, even storms can be and are victims. However, the media, society, and people in general will seek out, sensationalize, and even create victims in order to exploit them for political or financial gain. Or perhaps only to engage the "poor pitiful me" cycle so we can all feel crappy together. I must admit, on the surface I can see how people get caught in this trap; it gives you a sad story to tell over and over. Other people may express and show you compassion, maybe even feel sorry for you. The problem is, it attracts more of the same and the loop of sorrow and wallowing begins.

When these unhealthy messages begin to enter your mind or someone tries to label you a victim, have the discipline to say *hell, no*! Quietly shut down the "poor pitiful me" syndrome, turn your back on this destructive cycle, and choose to be empowered.

The way you think about and approach any situation or perceived obstacle ultimately determines your overall experience. So, if need be, adjust your approach. It doesn't matter how bad things get, there is always something to be thankful for. Pay attention to *that* stuff.

ћ

Chapter 11

Keep Showing Up

Success doesn't motivate me as much as integrity does. Everyone loses. I enjoy the pressure of showing up every single day, being focused, putting forth my best effort, getting the best out of my teammates, and enjoying the journey.

—Becky Sauerbrunn

My friend Bryan has two sons who were wrestlers at a local high school here in Oklahoma. The elder, Will, wrestled at 195 lbs. The younger, Josh, wrestled at 220 lbs. and was runner-up state champion in his weight class his sophomore year. Remarkably, at the young age of fifteen he was the toughest kid in his entire high school—he's a little wild and has a motor that will not quit; he just keeps coming at you. Will, being the older of the two, was forced to get used to a reversal of the normal older-brother–younger-brother dynamic. He handled it well, but it certainly wasn't easy.

After Josh won runner-up his sophomore year, he set his sights on becoming state champion his junior year, which was his brother Will's senior year. Let's just say, in

Oklahoma being a wrestling state champion is a *big* deal. The day came for the state finals to begin. Both Will and Josh qualified for their respective weight classes and would be going for the big prize. Everyone expected Josh to make the finals and have a shot at being a state champion, and he did not disappoint. The surprise came when Will defeated his opponent in the semifinals, giving him a chance to win the coveted title as well.

The championship round was about to start. As wrestlers in the upper weight classes, Josh was to wrestle in the final match and Will just before in the next-to-last match. We were all there to support our friend's sons as they tried to become champions. You could cut the energy in the arena with a knife.

Will stepped up to wrestle first. His opponent, who was a runner-up champ the prior year, looked like a member of SEAL Team 6. No matter. Will was ready to go.

"Let's do this!" Bryan hollered right next to me. We were both very nervous (okay, Bryan was a basket case). We knew what a win could mean for Will. The whistle blew and the match was on.

Both wrestlers looked good in the first and second periods, but after some intense back-and-forth action, the match ended in a 4-4 tie. During the first overtime, whoever scores first, wins. Will fought off what seemed to be a sure takedown to remain tied at the end of the first overtime. As the whistle blew to start the second overtime, both wrestlers were at the point of total exhaustion. Will was on bottom, the whole gym was screaming, and we could feel the win slipping away. Then, with mere seconds left in the match, Will kicked his hips out, hit a Peterson roll, and scored a four-point move to become an Oklahoma STATE CHAMPION!

The whole place erupted in a frenzy of emotion. There were tears of joy and relief. High fives and hugs were exchanged by men, women and kids alike. People who didn't even know one another were embracing and celebrating this young man's incredible upset victory. I have been around this sport much of my life, and this was the most inspiring win I had ever witnessed. It was truly an epic moment for all.

Bryan collapsed after Will's win. I helped him up, and I will never forget what he said to me. With tears streaming down his face, he looked at me and said, "This is the first tournament Will has ever won." Can you imagine? Will won only one tournament in his whole high school career and it was the state championship—the very last match of his senior year. Truly amazing! What a time to rise to the occasion.

Will completely pulled all the air out of that gymnasium with his performance. The only problem was, Josh still had to wrestle. He did not disappoint. He too won the state champion title that he'd worked so hard for and wanted so badly.

It was amazing to see the dynamic between the two brothers. Josh trained so hard and was so consumed, driven and determined to be a state champion. By continuing to show up and do the work, big brother Will was able to feed off this energy and unrelenting expectation of victory, in order to capture his own gold medal.

Soon after, Will was accepted to West Point Military Academy, where he currently attends and is a member of the rugby team. Josh, after winning a second state championship medal in his 2019 season, will attend and wrestle heavyweight for the distinguished University of Oklahoma wrestling program. These young men are shining examples of what can be accomplished with direction and no-quit determination.

As I write this story of these dedicated young men, I am taken back to my first memories of wrestling and the coach who tried to turn us into ten-year-old Marines. Crazy as he was, I now realize that he too played a big part in showing me how to reach for another level of "hammer down."

Whether your focus is sports, academics, family, friends, or your career, think and act like a champion. Have the dedication, determination, and even the relentless expectation to reach your goals and to be successful.

In this rapidly changing modern world of instant gratification, most people are not willing to put off the big prize while they apply effort to reach it. They want what they want, and they want it right damn now. They may get a token reward, what they think is a good prize, but the grand prize comes after you apply effort in a focused and determined fashion. That's where the really good stuff is. Most highly successful people will tell you that it was not talent or brains but desire, determination, and grit that were responsible for their success. Be willing to do the work; take consistent, determined action and power-step your way toward your goal.

If success were to come down to just one thing, it would be this: SHOW UP. Be willing to do the work. Do this—and keep doing this—and that alone will carry you far. Just like the story of Will, who kept showing up to practice with his younger—but bigger and meaner—brother. When things get tough and you want to give up, keep showing up, grind through the tough times, and see what can be learned. Remember that everything is feedback. Keep showing up and keep entering feedback—failures, successes, all of it—into your "computer" so you will continue to learn, adapt and grow.

Keep showing up and keep imagining yourself successfully having, doing or being whatever your imagination has created—your goal—and you will not be denied. The brain is like a supercomputer calculating the fastest and most efficient path toward what our mind creates. This applies to both the good and the bad; all input is stored and factored.

Consider something simple like picking a golf ball up off the ground. You don't stop and think about all the things you need to do, like bend at the knees and hips, open your hand or extend your arm. You get the picture; you just bend over and pick it up. Your mind knows everything and just does it. Or perhaps consider something a little more complex, like throwing a football to a receiver running down field. Your supercomputer kicks in. It begins to calculate the speed that the receiver is running, the wind velocity on the field, the position of the defenders, the air pressure of the ball in your hands, the force and direction needed—all these and many, many other details are factored by your brain in a fraction of a second. It's a pretty remarkable tool that we carry around with us every day.

Consider this as well: When teaching myself to play something new and difficult on the guitar, in the beginning I have to think slowly and look at each chord, finger placement and strumming pattern. I must slowly and meticulously feed this song into my brain, or my supercomputer, again and again. I do this over and over for a few days, many times a day, until I can do it without looking or thinking about it. After a while of practicing at this level, if I go back and try to look at the chords while I play, I will be hindered and slowed down.

Once you get all the information programmed into your brain, you have to move your mind out of the way, stop thinking, and just let the brain do its thing. Obviously, the more you practice, the more feedback that gets stored for your computer to factor in the next time you perform this task. This is the remarkable power we carry with us that can be applied to anything. Our brain automatically remembers what worked and what did not work from past attempts, then adjusts accordingly, without our even thinking about it, until it becomes firmly implanted in our mind and can then be executed in an effortless fashion.

Your mind has incredible power—when it has a task to unleash on. That is the key: it must have a goal, a direction. As discussed throughout this book, if the brain does not have a clear target or goal it can become a lazy, inefficient and destructive force. This is when boredom and negativity are allowed entry into your thoughts—from not having a plan.

Leverage this understanding; you have the tools. All of the techniques described here can help you tap into this incredible source of knowledge, power and energy. Like throwing the football with the right stimuli and feedback, success at anything can become almost automatic and effortless. The image you hold of yourself in your mind will be manifested. Make that image successful and remarkable; become the champion of your life. Discover the amazing feeling that is harnessed by living with purpose and passion.

Of course the first step is to show up, and once you do that, the ingredients are here for you: set master goals, execute on your power steps, develop spiritual balance, manage your mind, and all the other leverage methods discussed—they only need to be applied with fire and determination.

You are the fire, the positive energy needed to get these ingredients activated. Applying consistent pressure over time is how diamonds are created.

Conclusion

Tomorrow is . . . perfect when it arrives and it puts itself in our hands. It hopes we've learned something from yesterday.
—John Wayne

To conclude I must return to the beginning, to the grandfather I never knew, Grandpa Haley, who died when I was three. I would later find out that this short but sturdy man born in the 1890s worked on steam engines. He served his country, first by joining the Navy and then the Army when World War I started. He fought in France and helped save fellow comrades in the famous 1918 Battle of Argonne Forest. This stout gentleman could do a backflip wearing work boots well into his sixties. He could also catch and fry a flathead catfish like no other.

On the other side of the family is our Grandpa Andy, or Gramp. He was a real cowboy, as they say. He always said he broke his first horse at age five, and I was there to see him break his last one at the remarkable age of eighty-two. When Gramp was a toddler, his father would set him on the bare back of green colts that he would lead with him as he rode out to check the cattle. Gramp said, "At some point during the day my dad would just flip me the lead rope and there I went." He was the last of the cattle drovers west of the Mississippi River. He was a Spanish gentleman and a great friend and was considered "Gramp" by many. My brothers and I are very fortunate that he really was ours.

My grandmothers, too, were wonderful. Grandma Haley, who stayed at church that fateful day when my grandpa passed away, was my guardian angel. Her love and kindness were life-giving. Grandma Mary, Gramp's wife, was a saint—sweet, introverted, and quiet, but also *tough* and focused on her family. The incredible heartfelt love and grace that these two grandmothers displayed could fill a whole library of books.

These folks never stood on any championship podium or received any first-place trophies. But what I learned from my parents, grandparents, and others like them is that not all champions and heroes receive accolades or get medals. I learned that virtue is key to happiness. The work we do, the people we touch and the acts we commit will be our legacy. I learned that life is a gift meant to be lived with honor and faith, and, God willing, when it's all over, some piece of our best will carry on.

Hammer down. This term was used often throughout my youth. Perhaps you too now understand what it means: to act with intense purpose, drive and determination. Most of the time, "hammer down" involves the unleashing of high intensity focus and action toward an objective. But it also means accessing prayer, meditation, and the feeling of peace and connection. It means accepting responsibility—without beating yourself up—and making the choice to start again. It means letting go of the past and learning to live in the now. It means finding balance, harmony and respect in your life. All of this is "hammer down."

My sincere wish is for you to thrive and to enjoy your precious short time on this earth and help others do the same. I truly hope you will find my suggestions practical and useful in your everyday life. Thank you for allowing me to share some of my stories and misadventures with you, and for being part of my journey. May peace, happiness and success be your companions as you travel through this amazing adventure we call life.

Hammer down, friend.

Acknowledgments

I would like to thank a few people who have inspired me and provided valuable feedback throughout the writing of this book. In no particular order, a big "Thank You" goes out to Rich Hull; Casey McCormack; Joe, Braden and Blane Culp; Bryan, Will and Josh Heindselman; Major Ed Pulido; Stoney LaRue; Tony Kroutil; Blake McClure; Cory Benton; Brad Vincent; Mark Geuthle; Ken Ludwig; Kevin and Cora Beth Taylor; Chaz Richards; Cecil Noble; Chris and Keri Cochran; Charles and Vicki Daughety; Ron Gregory; Kent Shoemaker; Wes White; Larry Thomas; Jeff Tebow; and Doug Von Tungeln for being the first to buy five copies of this book before it was even finished.

I must also give a shout out to my brothers, Tim, Rick, and Randy Haley, as well as my extended family, Barbara, Laura, Danny, Dacin, Dusty, Darcie, Payton, Mason, Emma, Sonya, Rance, Desirae, Rhett, Madison, Megan, Amelia, Lacy, and Dalton—how lucky we all are to have each other!

To my gifted editor Karin Wiberg of Clear Sight Books. Her considerate way with people and skill with the written word helped bring this book to life. Thank you, Karin. You're the best!

To my amazing parents, Henry and Edwina Haley—thank you for your love and support, the example you set and the blessed family you created.

About the Author

K.P. HALEY resides in Oklahoma, where he enjoys sports, spending time at his ranch, playing his guitar, and having fun with family and friends. Raised on a working cattle ranch, K.P. went on to a successful thirty-year career in sales, marketing and investing before partnering in his own insurance agency, which he eventually sold to pursue other interests (the creation of this book among them!).

K.P. dives into the techniques and methods he has acquired over his life and working career—life lessons learned through his hunger for knowledge and his many years in search of wisdom and understanding. These lessons will transform those who embrace them.

K.P. (right) and his son, Dalton

CPSIA information can be obtained
at www.ICGtesting.com
Printed in the USA
BVHW031906151119
563990BV00002B/2/P

9 781734 051902